Silverstone
The Story of Britain's Fastest Circuit

Silverstone
The Story of Britain's Fastest Circuit

Peter Carrick

PELHAM BOOKS

First published in Great Britain by PELHAM BOOKS LTD
52 Bedford Square, London WC1B 3EF
1974

© 1974 by Peter Carrick

ISBN 0 7207 0717 X

*Set and printed in Great Britain by
Tonbridge Printers Ltd, Peach Hall Works, Tonbridge, Kent
in Garamond eleven on twelve point on paper supplied by
P. F. Bingham Ltd, and bound by James Burn
at Esher, Surrey*

CONTENTS

ILLUSTRATIONS

Between pages 96 and 97

Maps (from page 163)

ACKNOWLEDGEMENTS

No one person could possibly know the whole history of Silverstone. I have therefore drawn on the experiences and memories of many people closely associated with the circuit over the years since 1948. In particular I am indebted to Jimmy Brown, Peter Clark, Tony Salmon, Desmond Scannell, Rodney Walkerley, Rob Walker and Martyn Watkins for their willingness to search their memories and files on my behalf and for their patience and understanding in answering my questions.

My special thanks are also expressed to the staff resident at Silverstone for their time and energy in checking details.

Others who provided assistance and to whom I express appreciation are the Press and Public Relations Department and the Motor Sport Division of the Royal Automobile Club with particular reference to Neil Eason-Gibson, Ernest Hooley and Gordon Pearce; John Player & Son; the magazines *Autocar; Autosport, Competition Car, Motor, Motoring News* and *Motor Sport;* the Air Historical Branch of the RAF; the Auto-Cycle Union and the British Motor Cycle Racing Club; Leslie Nichol and the *Daily Express* and the many people too numerous to mention.

Especially do I appreciate the privilege extended to me by the Royal Automobile Club and the British Racing Drivers' Club, both of whom allowed me complete access to their confidential records and minutes of early meetings. The author is grateful to William Kimber & Co. Limited for permission to use an extract from *A Turn of the Wheel* by Stirling Moss, to Weidenfeld & Nicolson for permission to use an extract from *Prince of Speed* by Phil Read, and to the Hutchinson Publishing Group Limited for permission

to use extracts from *British Grand Prix* by Richard
Hough, *On the Grid* by Peter Garnier, *Destination
Monte* by Peter Harper and *Life at the Limit* by
Graham Hill.

Peter Carrick
Henlow
Bedfordshire

PICTURE CREDITS

*United Press International – Pictures 2, 3, 14; Daily Express –
Pictures 4, 5, 10, 19, 26; T. C. March – Pictures 7, 17a, Sport
& General – Pictures 8b, 16; B. F. E. Clark – Picture 11; John F.
Hughes – Picture 15; Harold Barker – Picture 18; Phipps Photo-
graphic – Pictures 20, 21, 24a, 24b, 25; D.P.P.I. – Picture 23.*

Foreword

It seemed appropriate, when asked by Pelham Books in the autumn of 1972 to give our blessing to a book they wanted to publish about Silverstone, to link this with 1973's Silver Jubilee Celebrations for the twenty-fifth year of the circuit's existence.

When we met the author and learned of the depth of research he wanted to carry out, we realised that publication in 1973 would be impossible and took the view that a good book at any time is preferable to an inferior job rushed through for a deadline.

I hope the public will share my view that Peter Carrick has written a very good book indeed, steering a well-judged course between solemnity and levity. Many incidents in the history of Silverstone have indeed been hilarious, and any over-emphasis of these aspects would have made us look like a bunch of irresponsible amateurs. Conversely, over-emphasis of the business of decision-taking, in what is potentially a significant group of commercial companies, could make it appear that we have lost the spirit of burning enthusiasm which in fact still motivates us.

It took the British Racing Drivers' Club nearly twenty years to succeed in buying the freeholds of Silverstone. I hope and believe that as landlords we are quite unique, in the sense that by the terms of our constitution we cannot distribute dividends: thus all our earnings, from the various operating companies which we own, are ploughed back into improving the Estate, for the benefit of the sport which we love and of the public whose ever-increasing support of our race meetings makes the whole thing possible.

Gerald Lascelles
President
British Racing Drivers' Club

1

Racing comes to Silverstone

Not since the thundering, epic days of pre-war Brooklands had there been such drama and sensation. Stimulated by the prospect of seeing a British Grand Prix for the first time ever, a huge crowd said to be well in excess of 100,000 had descended on a converted wartime airfield close to the slumbering Northamptonshire village of Silverstone.

Until that day – October 2, 1948 – Silverstone was unknown. Yet that particular Saturday saw the rebirth of international motor racing in Britain and Silverstone hailed as its Messiah.

The day was grey at first, but cloud soon yielded to clear sky and sunshine. From the early hours crowds had been arriving and the enclosures filled with an excited public. Desolate a week before, the former airfield was now black with people. Twenty-five racing cars, positioned on the starting grid, cracked with life. The massive crowd hushed as Lord Howe raised the Union Jack, held it outstretched for a moment, then brought it down strongly. It was a moment in a million as exhausts snarled and cars surged forward.

As they raced past the pits en route for Woodcote, Baron Emanuel de Graffenried urged his Maserati 4CL into the lead. At the corner it was de Graffenried, Leslie Johnson in the E-type ERA and Louis Chiron in a 4.5 Lago-Talbot huddled close, with Chiron sneaking into the lead as they pulled out of the bend.

Then sensation! Spectators drew back instinctively as there was a mighty crack and a flurry of sparks. Johnson and the ERA were out of the race, victims of a smashed universal joint. The free-flying half shaft ripped a hole in the fuel tank but Johnson, sensing the potential danger, jerked the car to and fro, freeing the axle before a spark could set the escaping fuel alight.

From that dramatic start the race had its share of incident and adventure. A flying stone struck Reg Parnell in the face and then a second stone kicked up and caught the tank of his Maserati with such force that the drain plug was ripped clean out of its rivets and fuel gushed onto the track. Incredibly, Parnell's Maserati had twice suffered a split fuel tank during practice.

An over-enthusiastic Duncan Hamilton brought down three markers on one corner and at Seaman spun round completely, but carried on. Bob Ansell put his Maserati into an elegant about-face, and the seasoned Luigi Villoresi also overdid Seaman Corner, crashed through a barrier, stopped, regained the track, and drove on.

Sparkle-eyed by a feast of racing the like of which had been denied them for years, the crowd observed the greatest drama of the day on lap 22 when Geoff Ansell crashed his ERA into the barrier at Maggotts. The car rose high and then rolled over, but a shaken Geoff survived the incident and seemed little worse for the experience.

On that first lap, Chiron's light-blue Talbot pulled into the lead, with Parnell hugging his tail, followed by Philippe Etancelin in another Lago-Talbot, and then Bira in the blue and yellow, new-style Maserati close behind. Alberto Ascari, No. 11, and Villoresi, No. 18, were already streaking through the field at electrifying speed.

In the early stages, drivers pushed their cars hard and some paid the penalty. Bira, up among the leaders for a third of the race, gradually fell behind because of fading brakes and it was brake trouble which forced out Gianfranco Comotti's Talbot, and others. Tough, unremitting Silverstone was already showing its teeth. The engine of Tony Rolt's Alta was in poor shape and the car wasn't seen after lap 6. Two laps later and a leaking tank gave Gordon Watson in the Alfa no alternative but to retire.

Raymond Mays, 1948 British hill-climb champion, had been seen as a strong British contender but he had to pull in his D-type ERA for a plug change, was forced into another stop a few laps later, and after starting again went out permanently with a broken piston. Baron de Graffenried, optimistically among the group to rush into Woodcote on that first, eventful lap, was down the field after ten, the result of an overheating engine, and was to finish the race in ninth position. The Baron only had to wait a year for his moment of glory for he was to return to

Silverstone in 1949 and, soft helmet pulled closely round his head and face in the tradition of the old time gladiators, pushed his Maserati consistently quicker than anyone else on the day to win Silverstone's second Grand Prix.

But in this inaugural meeting, only twelve of the twenty-five robust starters were to battle through to the end of the punishing 65-lap, 250-mile race.

Against formidable Italian opposition from pre-war star Luigi Villoresi to new boy Alberto Ascari in their latest 1½-litre two-stage-supercharged Maseratis with their low-built tubular frames and coil-spring suspension, British drivers in their vintage and more traditional ERAs laboured. In the early stages of the race they were well outpaced as the Italians, tyres screeching, negotiated the 3.8-mile circuit at an exhilarating average of more than 74 mph.

British drivers Parnell and Hamilton, also driving Maseratis, were well in touch briefly at the start, Hamilton even going ahead of the French driver Chiron at one point to take the lead, but by lap 3 the Italians took command, moving to the front and staying ahead for the whole of the race.

By lap 5 Villoresi and Ascari were involving their vivid, scarlet machines in a personal duel, putting up a great show to thrill and delight the crowd. Villoresi would lead, then Ascari. Both were passing and re-passing and dropping the rest farther and farther behind. Closest challenge came from Chiron in the Talbot, a couple of seconds behind but still going very well and fast.

Villoresi's fourth lap was to prove the fastest of the day, completed in 2 mins 52 secs at 76.82 mph. At the quarter stage the average was still up around 74.5 mph.

Oil and tyre deposits on the track were to slow down the cars in the later stages but, as the race developed, interest centred around the mechanics as the cars came in to refuel. While Villoresi refuelled from pressure hoses in 35 seconds and pit work for both Villoresi and Ascari was smooth, quick and efficient, other crews laboured with scant purpose, undisciplined and under-rehearsed. In contrast, Bob Gerard and his team worked smoothly. He took on thirty gallons of fuel, oil and water, and got the ERA away again in less than 45 seconds, sent off by rousing applause from the partisan crowd.

Villoresi refuelled at 27 laps and stopped again at 50. Ascari pulled in on 29 and again on 52. At half distance Villoresi led from Ascari, close to his tail, with Chiron in third position and Bira, in another of the latest Maseratis, in fourth place. The command of the front-running Italians was now obvious and although Villoresi slid and spun through oil patches on corners, Woodcote becoming particularly slippery, he looked fundamentally untroubled as, downfield, Chiron dropped out and further retirements allowed Louis Rosier through into third position. British interest now picked out Bob Gerard. Quietly, relentlessly and unspectacularly, he had been gobbling up the laps and now occupied fourth place.

It was a commendable and intelligent performance, but Bob was to do even better. With some twelve laps left, he overhauled Rosier to move into third position. Could he make a race of it with the Italians? It was a lot to ask, but Bob made a spirited challenge to Ascari. With his foot hard down he lapped once at 2 mins 58.2 secs and frequently at around 3 mins, but it wasn't enough to bring him close to Ascari.

The Italian's enforced change of rear wheels allowed his team mate Villoresi to go well ahead and even though the latter suffered a setback when his rev counter vibrated completely out of the dash, dropped to the floor and became wedged under the clutch pedal, he managed to hold out well. Even without a clutch the experienced Italian had enough in hand and on the last few laps even eased back to let Ascari close on him.

The Italians' Maseratis were the latest post-war versions of a remarkable marque. Their high-speed performances were much in advance of the best produced by the British cars, most of which were ten years old and had been kept in racing order, as *Motor* acknowledged by 'Herculean labours and by tuning, maintenance, replacement and repair'.

The British drivers, rightly, side-stepped a pitched battle with the more sophisticated Maseratis from the start. Their hopes were lodged in the plodding reliability of their cars and in the possible temptation of the Italians to overstretch the more temperamental engines of the Maseratis in the early laps. Gerard, in the immaculately prepared ERA, settled into eighth place and was content to stay there during the early laps, but it was a delight to note that both he and Peter Walker were at one point quicker through Woodcote than the Maseratis.

The Italians raced ahead, the end in sight. The vast crowd kept its enthusiasm and vigour, pressing forward as the leading cars came through to finish. It was Luigi Villoresi first at an average of 72.28 mph. Alberto Ascari was next at 72.19 mph, then to a rousing welcome came Bob Gerard, a magnificent performance to finish third at 71.54 mph. Rosier was fourth at 70.65 mph. Bira was fifth and John Bolster drove a remarkable race, moving through the field, to finish in sixth position.

The enormous crowd was difficult to control and even during the race, dangerous situations developed as spectators, stretching for a better view of the racing, infiltrated the course. Left largely to administer its own discipline, the crowd, to its credit, responded well and quickly to timely warnings put out over the loudspeakers.

In this respect, how dramatically different was this inaugural meeting at Silverstone from the present tight control of crowds and the repeated warnings at all circuits that motor racing is dangerous and that, as a member of the paying public, you are there at your own risk.

Though the Grand Prix had by definition been the highlight of a remarkable day when British motor racing was reborn, the entire occasion was a total success. First, that incredible crowd. Double the most optimistic estimate made by the RAC, it demonstrated so doubtlessly the huge following in Britain for big-time motor racing.

There was excitement, speculation and incident all the way, from long before racing began. First, disappointment when it was known that the Alfas and Ferraris, then dominating European Grand Prix racing, would be unable to appear because the Silverstone meeting had been timed too close to the important Monza race. Bad luck certainly, for the Alfas particularly were a big draw at any race meeting and would almost certainly have dominated Silverstone.

But this was a day that acknowledged little time for brooding. With the Alfas and Ferraris absent, the fastest and most exciting cars would be undoubtedly the new-type Maseratis. The Italians, Luigi Villoresi and Alberto Ascari, the latter the son of the famous driver of twenty years before, had entered. French stars were down to compete and there was a strong entry of British Racing Drivers' Club members. The Italians were to drive night and day to reach the circuit with their exciting 4CLT/48 Maseratis and arrived just in time for four laps of unofficial practice. As a result, they had to be content with a back position on the grid, even though Ascari had gone round fastest of all.

Incredibly, the desolation and bleakness of the wartime airfield had been transformed, fine testimony to the RAC who had worked almost night and day to get the place ready within just eight weeks. Here, now, for the first time in so many long years, was all the warmth, glamour, compelling atmosphere and excitement of a traditional Grand Prix. Two large grandstands overlooked the pit area; marshals and officials scurried around the starting grid; racing cars gleamed in the sunshine, exhausts barking; loudspeakers added their chatter; refreshment tents were besieged; and the enclosures thronged with an eager crowd. The BBC were there, ready for commentaries in the Light Programme at 1.50, 3.30 and 4.45.

The public could be admitted by car at £1 and £1.10 for parking, irrespective of how many people travelled in the vehicle. As someone said at the time: 'We shall find out at last just how many people an Austin 7 can manage to carry while just keeping moving!'

With the crowds still arriving, the day's first race, a 500 cc curtain-raiser, was flagged away after the legendary John Cobb, holder of the World Land Speed Record, had completed a ceremonial lap of honour in a new Healey Sportsmobile to open the circuit, escorted by distinguished motor cycle TT winners Bell, Frith and Cann.

The 500 cc category was for unsupercharged cars, popular since the war in hill-climbing and sprints, and this was the biggest event yet held in this category. In such a race the low capacity sprint tanks would be inadequate over the 13-lap, 50-mile race, and many of the brightly coloured little cars had, with great ingenuity, been fitted with larger tanks and were, of course, powered by units drawn from the motor cycle world.

The start was sensational, to be talked about years after. Did the starter's flag drop before the cars had been properly assembled? The crowd buzzed with speculation, but whatever the reason half the thirty starters paused on the line. Some made tentative moves, seemed to half-check, but then the race was definitely on and the cars were away.

An eighteen-year-old Stirling Moss, driving a Cooper JAP and fastest in practice, stormed from the line. Though favourite to win, Moss was led on the first lap by Strang in a powerful Vincent-HRD, but his very fast cornering regained him the lead on the second lap and, with relief, he saw what might have been his most serious challenge eliminated on the third as Strang's engine seized.

Meantime, the colourful and exuberant Spike Rhiando in his gold-painted Cooper JAP, after suffering a dismal start, was making astonishing progress through the field and on lap 4 was six seconds behind Moss, in second place. In a valiant effort to outdo Moss on Seaman Corner, Rhiando was lucky to survive a monumental slide, but when Stirling was forced to retire with transmission trouble, Rhiando was suitably placed and stormed on to finish first in 47 mins 10.6 secs at an average of 60.55 mph, in spite of a split tank that soaked him in petrol. John Cooper was second some six seconds later. Third in a Cooper was Sir Francis Samuelson who, according to that veteran authority Rodney Walkerley, had competed in the first Cyclecar Grand Prix of the ACF (Automobile Club of France), on the Amiens Circuit, in 1913 driving a Marlborough light car. The Cooper JAPs dominated the race, capturing five of the first six places.

Then came the big one, the Grand Prix, and because of the width of the track, five cars abreast made up the front rank, with alternate rows of four and five, with the two Italians, good humouredly, side by side on the sixth and last row. For motor racing fans in Britain, Silverstone was recapturing a lost magic and the tension and excitement built up strongly. The flag dropped and the race was on.

This first Grand Prix circuit start and finish was on the straight between Abbey and Woodcote. From there it ran along the perimeter track of the airfield to Woodcote, then on to Copse. A tight right-hander took it along the runway away from the perimeter and into the centre of the airfield to the runway intersection where a U turn led back to the perimeter track just short of Becketts. The circuit then followed the perimeter track, through Chapel and along Hangar Straight, to Stowe Corner, where a

sharp right-hander led back along another runway and back
to the centre intersection. A U turn round a tub took drivers
back to rejoin the perimeter road to Club Corner, then right to
Abbey and the home straight.

The map on page 163 illustrates the hazards of this first Silverstone circuit at the U turns. Only a line of tubs and flags
separated one U turn from the other so that when braking
fiercely to take the U turns cars were travelling at speed in
completely opposite directions, heading straight for each other.
The idea of the U turns was to make drivers brake strongly and
to pull them down to their lowest gear.

The Grand Prix was for cars of up to $1\frac{1}{2}$ litres supercharged
and up to $4\frac{1}{2}$ litres unsupercharged. The former would need to
stop to refuel while the heavier unsupercharged cars with their
bigger engines and higher capacity fuel tanks, would benefit
from a time advantage because they would be able to carry
sufficient fuel to run right through. Thus the race was poised
interestingly and in the excitement of seeing the Maseratis, the
absence of the Alfas and Ferraris was forgotten.

These latest Maseratis had six-cylinder engines with two overhead camshafts and four valves per cylinder. The new chassis
was lower, tubular, with quarter elliptic leaf springs at the
rear.

The French Talbots raced that day were also 1948 models,
single seaters with six cylinder pushrod engines, unsupercharged,
$4\frac{1}{2}$ litres, with light alloy head and block. They produced about
220 brake horse power at 4,200 rpm at 18 cwt unladen. The
fuel consumption on the Talbot was so good that they could
complete a 500 km Grand Prix non-stop.

More than the cars or the drivers, it was the occasion which
made this such a significant day in the history of motor racing in
Britain. How many people gained entry without paying is anyone's guess and no authenticated estimate of the number of
spectators was given, though the reported 130,000 was probably
over-optimistic. If it was difficult to get them all in it was just as
hard to get them all away again. Roads for miles around were
clogged for hours and even at midnight the circuit car parks were
still occupied.

Everyone was good-natured, for international racing in
Britain had been established once more and that was all that

mattered. Impromptu parties around camp fires were the perfect ending to a remarkable day, for no longer need Britain gaze enviously across the channel. No longer would there be overseas contempt for a country that couldn't run a big race. Silverstone had changed all that and from that day was to figure prominently in, and be central to, the motor race movement in Britain.

2

Finding a Home for
Motor Racing

In the summer of 1948, after three years of peace, Britain still
lacked a major motor racing circuit. Historic Brooklands had
died with the war and Donington Park, where the last full-scale
Grand Prix to be held in Britain had taken place ten years
before, was still securely under requisition by the War Office.

The country faced monumental post-war problems and motor
racing could muster little priority. As everyone struggled pain-
fully to pick up the pattern of normal living, discussion in the
somewhat august atmosphere of the Royal Automobile Club's
London headquarters in Pall Mall was about the indigenous
problems of the day, like buying a new carpet for the main hall,
making improvements and alterations to the kitchens, and decid-
ing how much could be spent on a gift for the Swiss Automobile
Club, due shortly to celebrate its fiftieth anniversary.

Yet having solidly taken root beneath these day-to-day issues,
festering quietly like an unseen and untreated sore, was the
RAC's bewildered dismay at the abysmal state of racing in peace-
time Britain and their unsuccessful attempts to do anything about
it. As the governing body of motor sport in the country they had
been unable to find a replacement for Brooklands and Donington,
those famous pre-war venues, in spite of all their efforts. This
impoverished state of affairs meant that fine motoring bodies
like the Junior Car Club, for instance, were forced for lack of
facilities nearer home to travel to places like St Helier, Jersey, to
run their races. The Channel Islands, Ulster and the Isle of Man,
along with most continental countries, did not suffer as the UK
did from a Parliamentary Statute which did not permit public
roads to be closed for car or motor cycle racing, although pedal

cycle racing was permitted – an anomalous situation which persists to this day.

Sharing the RAC's bitterness at the absence of a good race circuit was the British Racing Drivers' Club, whose members were being forced to do all their racing abroad. The BRDC, as early as November 1945 and already acutely aware of a critical situation developing as the future of Brooklands looked bleak, made a strong effort to have its voice heard in the debate on the future of Britain's most famous race circuit. They agreed to buy shares in the Brooklands' company solely to give them speaking time at the firm's next and crucial annual general meeting: and a year later, members were joining those of the Junior Car Club at a special protest meeting held to oppose the impending sale of Brooklands.

Later, with efforts to salvage the doomed Brooklands abandoned, with the Government adamant against the de-requisition of Donington, and with the untiring efforts of many legendary pioneers of pre-war motor racing in Britain still short of success, the BRDC's President, Lord Howe, was forced to the dismal admission: 'We in this country are still denied a venue for motor racing events and prospects for racing in Britain are not good.'

In the meantime, motor racing on the continent was buoyant and fast-developing. Fine, sweeping circuits, many on public roads, in France, Belgium, Italy and other countries had been back in use almost before the sound of the final wartime siren had died away, with the result that in the technical development of cars and in fast-driving technique and experience, Britain was struggling against uneven odds. Yet the potential for motor racing in Britain was vast and there was the promise of support on a generous scale from the *Daily Graphic* for the first post-war International race to be held in England.

Everyone, it seemed, was aware that the motor car was to be the first massive phenomenon of the post-war world – and was to prove the most durable. You did not need a crystal ball to predict the development of motor racing as a sporting giant with vast investment and national prestige at stake. Yet the Government would not budge. They held grimly to the few venues which would give motor racing in Britain a home.

So angered and frustrated was the BRDC committee that in

March 1948 it proposed and agreed a strong representation to the CIGS Field Marshall Viscount Montgomery. They would ask him for definite information on the future of Donington Park and push their claim for a sporting home for motor racing by obtaining the signatures of their members, and those of members of all motor sporting clubs in the country who had served under Monty in the war, on a petition expressing their disfavour and concern.

In the midst of the gloom there was a glint of hope when the secretary of the BRDC, Desmond Scannell, met the Clerk and members of the Corporation of Barrow-in-Furness in Lancashire to discuss the possibility of establishing a race circuit on Walney Island aerodrome, with Corporation backing. It was later announced that the Barrow-in-Furness Corporation had agreed to the club's proposals to hold a race meeting on Walney Island, but a ruling from the Ministry of Civil Aviation was still awaited.

It looked promising, but behind the scenes more significant action was taking place. To those most concerned Lord Howe revealed details of an aerodrome he had inspected in the Midlands, with runways and a perimeter track, which he considered very suitable for racing. The idea of converting an airfield into a motor racing circuit was not new. The possibilities had been demonstrated immediately following the end of the war when speed trials were held on the Elstree aerodrome runway. There was a huge entry and a remarkably enthusiastic crowd of over 30,000, in spite of petrol rationing. There were also the intervarsity meetings remembered by Rodney Walkerley and held on a circuit at Gransden Lodge, one of the many Suffolk airfields around Mildenhall, when a feature of the long programme of short races was an event for vintage racing cars, establishing a trend which was to continue for many years.

For a while, little happened, but then events moved swiftly. It was well known that the RAC, the BRDC and other organisations had pursued with vigour the possibilities of racing round airfields and a number of disused aerodromes had been inspected and the likelihood of racing there assessed. First hope of a breakthrough was voiced at a specially-convened meeting of the RAC executive committee on July 21, 1948. Chairman Lord Howe explained that the meeting had been called to 'consider a matter of importance and urgency by reason of the fact that a decision by the executive committee was necessary for the guidance of the competitions committee.'

Lord Howe reminded members of the efforts that had been made to secure a suitable site for motor racing, but for one reason or another, he said, no suitable site could be found . . . 'until now.' Within just a few short seconds he delivered in private the most heartening news for motor sport in Britain for more than a decade, reporting how it had been tentatively arranged that a short term lease from July 1948 for one year could be obtained from the Air Ministry of Silverstone Aerodrome, near Towcester, with an option of extension.

It was exciting news, but events forced the pace on decisions. There could be no lengthy deliberation or the opportunity might be lost, for Lord Howe further revealed that if speedy agreement could be reached there should be just time for all necessary arrangements to make Silverstone the venue for the 1948 RAC Grand Prix on a date reserved for this event in the International Sporting Calendar.

It was a thrilling and tempting opportunity, but snap decisions are alien to the basic nature of governing bodies, however worthy; and besides the possibility raised fundamental issues. For a start, it would be a prodigious job with so little time in which to do everything, but even more significantly the RAC would need to take on the responsibility of running the circuit itself . . . and that was something it had not done before. Indeed, the committee reminded itself, it was no part of the RAC's responsibility to run tracks and Colonel Browne pointed out that in the past the RAC, acting as the jockey club of motor sport, had not itself been concerned in the financing of racing tracks.

Was it necessary for the RAC to do so now? Lord Howe said he felt it was. 'If advantage was to be taken of the Air Ministry offer it was necessary for the RAC to take responsibility in this connection as the offer could not be made to any other interest,' he said. 'Furthermore,' he went on, 'if the RAC Grand Prix is to be held this year an immediate decision to the Air Ministry's favourable offer was essential.'

In retrospect the debate may seem to have been irrelevant and a waste of time. Surely this was the very opportunity for which everyone in motor racing had been clamouring. What was there to decide?

Issues have the habit of becoming clearer with the passing of time, but in July 1948 the RAC, as later events were to prove, had to be cautious of its own position in the organisation of motor sport in Britain. Fundamentally, it was not for them to invest money in motor racing circuits; they had no such mandate, but here was undoubtedly a golden opportunity which might benefit motor racing for many years to come.

The temptation grew as Lord Howe reported that, on a visit he would shortly be making to Berne, he would be in a position to contact various famous international racing drivers who might have great spectator value in the RAC Grand Prix. By this time the committee had almost sold itself on the idea, but supposing they agreed to go ahead, was there really sufficient time to make all the arrangements for an event as important as a Grand Prix? What about spectator accommodation, the organisation of the pit areas, the hundreds of officials necessary and the scores of services required? A course would have to be worked out, fencing material ordered and erected; there would be the need for complicated insurance cover, the allocation of prize money.

The problems were obvious, the task monumental, but the hunger to see big-time motor racing once more in Britain was strongest of all and won the day. After further discussion the committee agreed for the short-term contract with the Air Ministry to be implemented 'subject to suitable terms being arranged through the club's solicitor, the financial aspects of the matter being considered by the club's auditor, and the assurance of the competitions committee at their meeting within the month, that there would be sufficient time to stage the Grand Prix on the date decided.'

Silverstone, as we were to come to know it, was on the way and *Autocar* asked joyously if cautiously: 'Airfields for Racing this Year?' Motor racing apart, the establishment of Silverstone was vital as a testing and proving ground for racing and production cars in the vanguard of a swiftly expanding British motor car industry and it was the unique sense of tradition at Silverstone, allied to its all-purpose nature as a racing and testing circuit, that was over the years to set it apart from other tracks to be set up in the country.

A new and exciting era was about to begin for the small

Northamptonshire village. Until the establishment of an airfield close by during the war, and again briefly after its closure, there had been little to disturb the rural calm of Silverstone. Sited in Whittlebury Forest, its name is said by one source to be derived from 'silva tone', meaning wood town, and Silverstone certainly has always had plenty of timber yards. Until the reign of Edward I there was a royal hunting lodge there and it was also significant for Luffield Priory. In fact, inside the circuit at Abbey Curve there remain the foundations and ruins of the Priory of Luffield and between the corners at Becketts and Chapel, racing cars scream by the site of the chapel of St Thomas a Beckett. A pre-historic burial ground is sited at the edge of the club straight.

The war came late to Silverstone. The RAF station was opened on March 20, 1943, and officially became what in service jargon is termed 'a surplus, inactive station' in October 1947. For most of its operational life it was occupied by 17 Operational Training Unit, training crews for the RAF using Wellingtons.

When the RAF moved out, Silverstone was left to rot, abandoned to a thousand echoes and memories of a wartime which had its own special glamour and excitement. Paint peeled off woodwork; grass began pushing its way through gaps in the concrete; a door here and there banged against its hinges. It was this derelict and uncharitable sight which greeted a small party of early visitors to Silverstone shortly after the RAC had completed the vital negotiations for its short-term use. Rodney Walkerley remembers: 'It was a dreary day when I went with a Press party and the RAC to Silverstone for the first time, grey and rainy and there was the usual cold wind which generally blows across airfields. The general impression was that it was a desolate place, but better than nothing.'

In spite of the daunting prospect the desolate Silverstone must have presented in 1948, a little imagination was sufficient to appreciate what Silverstone could become. In many respects it was ideal for motor racing. Positionally, it was the best of all the airfields contemplated, being within comparatively easy travelling distance from London and the Home Counties, and virtually on the doorstep of the large population areas of the Midlands, so closely linked industrially and economically with motor car manufacture. To the RAC's early adventurers, the potential was obvious and clear, even though at that time they might not have gone quite so far as Richard Garratt was to write retrospectively: 'The greatest days of the old airfield were yet to come.' It must be remembered of course that the initial lease was for only twelve months and nobody was prepared to say what might happen after that.

For a start, the degree of public support for this experiment was not known and some defeatists were already deploring the idea of attempting to run a Grand Prix round an airfield. It was against the traditions of the Grand Prix, they claimed, and such atmosphere and spectacle could not be summarily transplanted to the gaunt, bland expanse of an unknown airfield.

The RAC had little time to listen. Ahead of them was the herculean task of conversion, with the hampering restriction of temporary construction foremost in their minds. For this 1948 Grand Prix was perforce to be held on an ad hoc basis, its success or failure largely determining the course of future events.

Anticipating a green light on the proposed contract with the Air Ministry by the club solicitor, the RAC had already begun to plan their Grand Prix. Lord Howe had been in touch with certain car manufacturers and several famous international drivers; Professor Clements inspected the perimeter, track and runways and said some slight repairs would be necessary. And a sum of £1,500 recommended by the Competitions Committee for prize money was approved.

Time was frighteningly short, but the RAC kept its head and pushed ahead with its labours. As one observer remarked: 'One dominant impression after a visit to Silverstone last week was one of sheer bogglement at the magnitude of the task which by hook or crook the RAC has got to get through before October 2. How, apart from anything else, the purely physical part of the job – construction of the stands, rehabilitation of the existing buildings and so forth – is to be done in the time is almost beyond comprehension.'

Causing additional frustration were the administrative snags resulting from the boundary between Northants and Buckinghamshire bisecting the airfield. The odds in purely physical terms were against the Grand Prix taking place, as so much had to be done, but the crusade was on, the time for action was now and a fine spirit of co-operation prevailed. Volunteers were quickly seized upon and drafted into action. Motoring clubs gave their time and labour generously. Motoring journals offered to provide trophies. From straw bales to lavatories; from the allocation of expenses for the transportation of competing cars to the erection of grandstands and the installation of a public address system; from race control to crowd control, the check list was almost as long as the circuit itself.

If the volume of work could dictate success then this first post-war RAC Grand Prix was guaranteed the most lavish triumph, but in reality everything was done within the framework of speculation, impermanence, uncertainty and doubt. In spite of it all and the last-minute disappointment and crisis when the Ferrari and Alfa teams decided not to appear, the 1948 RAC Grand Prix took place, as history and Chapter 1 has recorded.

It was a turning point in the evolution of motor racing in Britain and the RAC's courage and far-sightedness were vindicated. The overwhelming success of the occasion brought its pioneers some of the glory they deserved. Reported an *Autocar* editorial: 'Auspicious revival of full-scale motor racing in England. Congratulations are due all round to those who made the event possible, and particularly to the RAC. Grand Prix racing in Britain is thus reborn and the aims of all must be to keep it alive.'

Almost before the cheers had died away, renewed doubts and suspicions were poking above ground, and centred around the RAC's role in taking over a racing circuit. When delegates of motoring clubs from all parts of the country held their annual conference with the RAC Competitions Committee in December 1948, a suggestion that the RAC intended to exercise a monopoly vis-à-vis airfields was vigorously repudiated. The RAC had to make it clear that Silverstone would be available for closed, invitation and open events organised by other affiliated and recognised clubs.

At this point Silverstone was not viewed with any degree of permanence, even by the RAC. A minute from the Annual General Meeting held on March 21 1949 read: 'Whilst by no means ideal, Silverstone provides a valuable stopgap either until

Donington becomes available or some other circuit is built to replace it.'

But in spite of the catalogue of hazards and obstacles to which it was subjected in ensuing years, Silverstone was to endure and flourish against uncommon odds, its life expectancy as a motor racing circuit often doubtful, but never extinguished.

3

The Early Years

Silverstone was established because of committed racing men like Lord Howe, Desmond Scannell, Wilfrid Andrews and Stanley Barnes, who took most of the responsibility for that first post-war Grand Prix. Their strong will, tenacity and sheer resolve to see Britain with a fine circuit of its own, dictated the course of events and fashioned success out of circumstances almost totally alien.

However, so the story goes, racing had come to Silverstone even before these stout-hearted trail-blazers had arrived on the scene. It all began in a Midlands pub on the evening of the Shelsley Walsh Hill Climb in September 1947, where competitors foregathered to re-live the dramas of the day. Present was Maurice Geoghegen, who lived in Silverstone and who had, naturally if perhaps unlawfully, gravitated to the airfield to test a racing car he had built the previous winter. As the evening developed, the idea of a few laps around Silverstone took root. Within such an atmosphere of conviviality, resolutions are often made with alarming ease and courage. The outcome was that the following day eleven chain-driven Frazer Nashes and a Bugatti descended unceremoniously on an unsuspecting Silverstone and there took place a race over a two-mile circuit and run in an anti-clockwise direction.

Silverstone was ill-equipped for such attention, and set in the middle of agricultural land, turned up a few natural hazards to racing in those premature days. The race had to be abandoned when sheep wandered unconcernedly on to the track.

This informal inaugural meeting has since become a Silverstone legend and was to be remembered later when bigger guns were brought forward to fire heavier armour in the battle for Silverstone.

If Maurice Geoghegan discovered Silverstone and crusaders like Wilfrid Andrews and Lord Howe established it as a race circuit, then Basil Cardew, Desmond Scannell and Tom Blackburn must rightfully take credit for its early development in those first days. The British Racing Drivers' Club had worked closely with the RAC in securing that initial lease which first brought racing to Silverstone and, having won that particular battle, immediately laid plans for more racing there. They had agreed to run an international meeting on August 20, 1949, but problems were developing over their inability to find backing for the event.

Basil Cardew, motoring correspondent of the *Daily Express,* and Desmond Scannell, secretary of the BRDC, knew each other well and Desmond confided his concern to Basil when the two met casually.

Basil hot-footed the news back to the *Express* and shortly afterwards phoned Desmond: 'Can you come for a meeting with Tom Blackburn?' he enquired. Desmond did not need pressing, for Blackburn was even then a powerful voice in the Beaverbrook camp, and when he and Tom Blackburn met they talked about the future of motor racing in Britain and the BRDC's immediate concern in finding support for the August event. It was an informal meeting, friendly and interesting, and at the end of it Blackburn promised the backing of the *Express.*

In these days of carefully-worded contracts and everything down on paper, it is astounding that for all the close liaison between the *Daily Express* and the BRDC at Silverstone in ensuing years, the agreement that started it all was sealed with a casual handshake, nothing more. As Desmond Scannell remembers: 'There was no agreement signed, not a single official piece of paper. Tom Blackburn merely said he would do it and he was a man of his word.'

Tom Blackburn, later to become knighted, was then general manager of the *Express.* He was a shrewd businessman and there is no doubt that he saw in the deal with the BRDC a means of promoting his newspaper to a mass audience. It was a publicity stunt and as a measure of the potential such a link would provide, he had the outstanding success of the RAC's Grand Prix of but six months before. In view of this it seems hardly credible that the BRDC had to go shopping for help.

That they did was fortunate for the *Express* as well as for the club and Silverstone. Their ties were to grow stronger with the passing years and Tom Blackburn developed a genuine fondness for the BRDC and the people in it. As his interest in motor racing grew he became a long-term benefactor, his personal contribution to racing at Silverstone going far beyond the call of normal duty.

In the meantime, the RAC was not dragging its feet. Conscious of the insecurity of tenancy at Silverstone and bolstered by the succees of 1948, they had already pushed ahead with plans for a 1949 Grand Prix, bringing it forward to May 14. This second Grand Prix was officially elevated to Grande Epreuve rank and given the title of British Grand Prix, a distinction which had already been colloquially conferred on the RAC's Grand Prix of the previous year. For 1949 the course was altered. The potentially dangerous U turns were eliminated and the runway was not used, except for a slow chicane which had been constructed at Club Corner. A lap was now three miles, the 100 laps of the Grand Prix giving a distance of just 300 miles.

From the start the RAC had been reluctant to accept the need for start money to attract the top drivers. Instead they spoke of expense money, but with German teams having been paid around £1,000 per car before the war to appear at Donington, the RAC's policy, though understandable because of the enormous expense in staging such a meeting, was unrealistic if the world's top drivers were to be tempted. Though prize money of £1,500 was offered for the 1948 Grand Prix, it was plain that the Ferrari and Alfa teams were absent because the money was not enough; and British drivers were expected to appear for nothing! The BRDC opposed the RAC on this issue and Lord Howe found himself in an awkward position, being president of the BRDC and also chairman of the RAC's competitions committee. He took the RAC view and it was only after the BRDC had made strong representations to him, with Des Scannell, Rodney Walkerley and others visiting him on his sick bed in his flat in Curzon Street, that he agreed with some reluctance to their views, and as a result starting money on something like the continental scale was for the first time agreed by the RAC.

But for 1949 the money again was not sufficient to tempt the

Ferrari and Alfa teams and the Maseratis were once more the major contenders. With Villoresi driving, an Italian victory was again anticipated, but this time the Italian's engine blew up and he was forced to retire. Bira's Maserati had a brake failure as he led the field and he was eliminated when he flew off the course, struck the straw bales and the car was too badly wrecked for him to continue. This left de Graffenried's Maserati in the lead, but, reminiscent of the '48 Grand Prix, Gerard in his faithful ERA was close at hand. Was a British victory possible? It seemed so as Gerard took one pit stop to Graffenried's two and began to shorten the distance. Ignition trouble then slowed him down and the Italian car raced ahead once more, though Gerard hung grimly to that second place, ahead of Louis Rosier in a Talbot.

The winning Maserati of de Graffenried completed the 300 miles in 3 hrs 52 mins 50.2 secs at an average of 77.31 mph. Gerard's average speed was 76.95 mph, but Bira's Maserati claimed the fastest lap at 82.82 mph. Again, Silverstone was besieged in the manner of the latter day pop festivals and the vast crowd, hungering for a British victory, had been brought to its toes by Reg Parnell, whose splendid career was to be so closely associated with Silverstone, when he held a good lead until his back axle ran out of oil. That he was driving a Maserati would not have diluted the strength of his victory, had he been able to hold out, for this excited crowd. Parnell was already a great favourite and was to drive many memorable races at Silverstone during his fine career.

Three months later the crowds were flocking back to Silverstone for the first *Daily Express* International Trophy Meeting, organised by the BRDC. The same course was used, but without the chicane, to give a distance of 2 miles 1,710 yards. The smooth professional publicity machine of the *Daily Express* had secured nationwide attention for the races and a massive crowd in excess of 100,000 converged on the circuit. The meeting was to signal the start of a completely new era of big-time motor racing in Britain. Tom Blackburn, once having committed his paper and his interest to Silverstone, was to be satisfied with nothing short of the best. For him and the BRDC the traditional running of a single major race was not enough. The idea was to promote a complete entertainment package, with several races run in close succession to one another. It imposed great strain on the marshals and stretched the entire organisation to the limits, but it gave the public the continuing excitement it wanted.

That first meeting was historic for it introduced production sports car racing to Britain. This 25-lap event produced the following winners: *General Category:* L. Johnson (Jaguar) 82.80 mph. 2nd: P. D. C. Walker (Jaguar). 3rd: N. Culpan (Frazer Nash). Class Results: *Over 2500 cc* – L. Johnson (Jaguar) 82.80 mph. *1501–2500 cc* – N. Culpan (Frazer Nash) 81.73 mph. *Up to 1500 cc* – E. Thompson (HRG) 70.89 mph. The Manufacturers' Team Prize was won by Healey with drivers Rolt, Chiron and Wisdom. Second place in the Under 1500 cc class was taken by Silverstone's present chief executive Peter Clark, in another HRG. The 500 cc Race was won by Brandon in a Cooper at 79.61 mph. Coopers driven by Moss and Dryden were second and third.

Among the entries for the main race were Italians Villoresi, this time in a V12 Ferrari, Farina in a Maserati, and Ascari in another Ferrari. A British win was out of the question, but the enormous crowd witnessed some spectacular racing with the Italians dominant. Alberto Ascari raced his Ferrari ahead of all competition and won at an average speed of 89.58 mph. Farina was second and Villoresi third. The fastest lap of the day was recorded during practice when Ascari's Ferrari and Bira's Maserati both reached 93.35 mph.

The first International Trophy Race meeting was a brilliant success and the public response to major motor races such as those now being staged at Silverstone was quite incredible. Pre-war race meetings had attracted crowds of 8–10,000. Brooklands on a good day could not do better than about 12,000 ('the right crowd and no crowding'), while Donington had only 50,000 to see the great German racing teams in 1937 and 1938. In comparison Silverstone's 100,000-plus was astronomical and carried with it all the evident excitement and tension that only a vast crowd can generate.

Clouding an otherwise superb International Trophy day was the fatal accident to 'Jock' St John Horsfall, the first death at Silverstone. In the main event he crashed his ERA at Stowe Corner. He hit the straw bales and the car overturned. Jock was a tenacious and brilliant driver whose epic 24-hour solo drive at Spa just a few weeks before, which gave him 4th place, was still being talked about. For the authorities Jock's death caused concern and a minute from a subsequent meeting of the BRDC, reads: 'The race was marred by the death of Horsfall and it is disquieting to recall that on three occasions at Silverstone, cars have overturned after striking straw bales.'

Shortly after, and arising directly out of Horsfall's fatal accident, the BRDC appointed a special sub-committee to look into the possibility of finding a substitute for straw bales, and the then BRDC Secretary, Desmond Scannell, remembers that there were so many conflicting reports of what happened that it was decided to have specially trained incident observers at future races – all senior police officers. Horsfall was a popular member of the BRDC. As a result of the tragedy the dinner which was to have been held on the Monday following the event was cancelled.

Overall, however, this first co-operation between the BRDC and the *Daily Express* was accepted by all concerned as an enormous success. As Desmond Scannell wrote in his report to the club's AGM the following March: 'We were able to promote what has been described as the most successful motor race meeting ever held in these islands – most successful both in the variety and quality of the actual racing and in the record attendance of some 110,000 spectators.' Basil Cardew said later: 'It was the sparkling combination of the *Daily Express* and the BRDC which placed motor racing on the map in Britain, and was to bring to the fore our own drivers to a position for many years unrivalled on the world's circuits.' Total gate money was more than £24,000, a considerable amount in 1949, and it was said that the *Daily Express* and the BRDC had hand-in-hand found themselves a financial bonanza. Hardly! In fact, with entertainment tax still very much part of post-war life in Britain and claiming £8,500 of the total stake, there was virtually nothing left over when all the expenses had been met. Entertainment tax, until its abolition in the mid-50s, was to remain a fearful burden for Silverstone. Said Desmond Scannell, recalling those days: 'We tried many times to get exemption from entertainment tax. An event had to be educational to qualify for exemption and all kinds of ways were tried to persuade the authorities that motor racing at Silverstone was in some way educational. But they just wouldn't have it ... and I suppose you can hardly blame them.'

Entertainment tax was to continue as an off-stage villian of the Silverstone show, ever-lurking in the shadows as a warning of the need for prudent organisation, even in those days of such magnificent attendances.

Of the 25s. received for a pits grandstand seat, 11/10 went on tax. Of the remaining 13/2 an average of 6s. represented the amount paid to the contractor for erecting the stand, which left a balance of 7/2 of the original 25s.

This illustrated one of the financial problems attendant on the organisation of a race at a venue devoid of any permanent installations. As was noted in committee at the time: 'Grandstands just for one meeting cost a disproportionate amount of money, as did the 101 other items which have to be provided.'

The organisation of such an event had similarities with a large-scale military operation and depended perhaps to a greater degree than now, on the countless numbers of willing helpers happy to give time and effort to the cause of motor racing. For that first *Express* Trophy meeting, over 1,000 persons were on duty. Fourteen doctors and 120 St John Ambulance Brigade personnel manned a tent hospital and eleven first-aid posts and dealt with over 600 cases. Such was the magnetic attraction of motor racing in this post-war surge of enthusiasm that it was not uncommon for a spectator to present himself at one of the first-aid posts, announce himself as a diabetic for instance, and request his regular injection. For Silverstone, it was all part of the service! Thus, within a year, the basic pattern of motor racing at Silverstone had been established and was to continue in years to come to hinge on the great British Grand Prix and the spectacular International Trophy meetings supported by the *Express,* who were also to help in promoting many of the early British Grands Prix.

That first year saw many other events and activities taking place at Silverstone. There was a successful motor cycle meeting organised by the British Motor Cycle Racing Club (Bemsee) and eight amateur motor clubs arranged race meetings and speed events. It was at club level that Silverstone was to prove so vital in the development of motor sport in Britain, for many new drivers were now able to gain valuable experience in the skills of race driving, competing against fellow club members. Even in the '70s Silverstone still has many amateur club events a year and it was this regard in the early days for the grass roots of the sport that brought it the reputation as the cradle of post-war motor racing in Britain.

Silverstone was also much in demand for individual tuning and testing purposes and even during that first year was the venue for a great deal of motor sport activity of all kinds.

Remarkably, the summer was excellent and every event was held in perfect weather. On October 13th, 1949, Stanley Barnes was able to report optimistically on Silverstone, revealing that the circuit had produced substantial revenue which would go towards the cost of the RAC's Competitions Department, then a considerable drain on the RAC's financial resources, and to the small resident staff at the circuit. He strongly recommended a continuance of the same basic policy, although at that stage the lease, due to expire in two months, had not been renewed and a further complication could be that the Ministry of Agriculture was due to take over the site.

Even so, demand for the use of Silverstone increased and all the clubs who staged meetings in 1949 came back with official requests for dates in 1950. In addition, the Auto-Cycle Union wanted two dates and it was known that many other clubs and organisations were clamouring for time at Silverstone.

With the tenancy of Silverstone finally secured for a further short term, the circuit inked in the dates, but by this time all the attention was on May 13, the date of the next British Grand Prix. Behind the scenes, outside the country, decisions were being taken which would confer a particular honour on Silverstone and motor racing in Britain. The FIA (Federation Internationale de l'Automobile) decided to bestow on the British Grand Prix the title of Grand Prix d'Europe. Never before had the honour of staging the Grand Prix d'Europe been given to this country and it was a noble gesture and an exciting recognition of what Silverstone had achieved and become in such a remarkably short time. This memorable occasion, which was attended by the King and Queen – the first time a British reigning monarch had witnessed a motor race – helped to make 1950 a magnificent year for Silverstone, for in addition a second *Daily Express* Trophy meeting in August attracted the biggest attendance of any event yet run in the country and among an excited crowd was His

Royal Highness the Duke of Edinburgh, who had attended the BRDC's 21st birthday celebrations in December 1948. Both occasions are described in some detail in the next chapter.

Having by now established itself as an exciting race centre, Silverstone was by no means set on a quiet, easy course with everything going for it. From those primitive and early days, as is shown in Chapter 9, it was beset with problems and difficulties, often concerned with tenancy and ownership. But it is probably from the rigours of its background and the need to face squarely many severe problems, that the special character of Silverstone emerged.

It is easy to forget in these days when motor racing in Britain takes place on a number of circuits, just how important were those early events at Silverstone. There was nothing even approaching their magnitude elsewhere and it is certain that the Silverstone policy of those late 40s and early 50s set the standard to which all future racing in Britain and in many countries abroad aspired.

Varied programmes, multi-race meetings and new standards of presentation and professionalism – all were seen for the first time at Silverstone, which was also the proving ground for British race car manufacturers. To this extent it is reasonable to assume that had not Silverstone been established when it was, the British cars which later dominated the motor racing scene would not have come about, for it was Silverstone which gave our engineers and designers the inspiration and the practical opportunity they needed.

These were pioneering days, remembered with affection, and in some cases with red faces in the light of subsequent events, by those who were part of them. There was a barnstorming sincerity about the undertaking and there was great response to the challenge of it all. Says Desmond Scannell: 'There was nothing approaching those early days at Silverstone. The public, starved of motor racing for so many years, used to arrive the night before, coming from as far as the West Country and from the far north of Scotland. Gates opened at 6 am. It was all enormous work and there were no precedents to work to, but the small corps of officials was supplemented by a mass of volunteers. These were the days when the timekeepers occupied an old bus and race control, helped on its way by Boy Scout volunteers, was located in an old cowshed. A doctor in Towcester was co-opted to run the medical services. Straw bales were the only protective measures we had. All installations had to be temporary as there was no permanent tenancy, and for the same reason no major investment could be allocated to lavatories and similar amenities which, to be admitted, were a little rugged in the early days. While there appears to have been little opposition to Silverstone developing as a race circuit from the people in the village, co-operation from other sides was not always forthcoming.'

Desmond Scannell remembers an early meeting with the police of both Northants and Bucks, called in an effort to ease the traffic congestion on race days. The environment had not come to terms with motor racing then, as it has today, and Scannell said that one of the senior Police Officers present said openly he saw Silverstone as a nuisance and that he would do whatever he could to get motor racing there stopped. And always there were niggling problems like trying to persuade the County Agricultural Committee to share the expense of additional fencing. Money – or the lack of it – was a constant concern to almost everyone associated with those early Silverstone meetings.

It is true to say that there was some criticism of the RAC's charges for the use of the circuit and concern at what was thought by some people to be the excessive profits likely to accrue to the RAC as a result. More than once the BRDC challenged the RAC on this and had the fee payable by the BRDC to the RAC reduced for 1949 from £3,252 as formally notified to BRDC by the RAC, to £2,500 – 'in the light of conditions now existing as regards the RAC's liabilities for the track.'

In two years time the RAC was to surrender its lease of Silverstone and the circuit moved into another era under the direct aegis of the British Racing Drivers' Club. It was, however, to be another eighteen years before the BRDC took over complete ownership of the circuit in 1970.

Such administrative changes held little interest at the time for the average enthusiast, who in the early 50s was far more excited at the prospect of seeing for the first time a strong British challenge on the track to the runaway victories of the Italians, and the ascendancy of the Ferraris over the previously all-conquering Alfas. There was also the unexpected drama of the *Daily Express* trophy meeting of 1951 which was abandoned because of a cloudburst, Reg Parnell being declared the winner amid a storm of protest and controversy. It was also in the early 50s that it was decided that retreads would not be acceptable on cars competing in any events organised by the BRDC and that crash helmets would become obligatory – two unspectacular decisions in themselves, but significant to the development of motor racing, and indicative of the BRDC's continuing leadership in the detail of race organisation.

The *Express* trophy race of 1950 was held on August 26 and the Alfas, after collecting the first three places in the Grand Prix with Farina, Fagiolo and Parnell, came home first (Farina) and second (Fangio) in the Trophy event. But time was fast running out for the mighty marque and in the Grand Prix the following year it was Ferrari who secured first and third places with Gonzalez and Villoresi, though Fangio took second place for Alfa. For the once illustrious Alfa Romeo, the halcyon days were gone and they were soon to leave the Grand Prix scene, elbowed out by the massive Ferrari assault.

The 1950 Trophy meeting also went down in history because of the debut of the BRM. The entire project, which was a Raymond Mays vision, had fired the imagination of the nation. Built on finance contributed by the British motor industry and by various individuals who wanted to see the Union Jack flying high at the world's race circuits, it was under-financed and over-complex, and was certainly not ready for competition when the sheer volume of public interest in the car virtually forced it on to the track in 1951, having first been scheduled to appear in 1949. The BRM performed a couple of demonstration laps in 1950 before the King and Queen at the Grand Prix d'Europe, and there was great enthusiasm and anticipation as it was publicised to appear at the *Express* 1950 meeting.

When it failed to show for practice there was intense speculation and drama. Last-minute problems threatened its appearance, but the BRDC and the *Express* were building their reputation on keeping faith with the public. If they said a car would race they would do everything possible to make sure it did. So an aircraft was hired and the BRM arrived at Silverstone about an hour before the start of the race, having been flown to a nearby airfield. What tension. What drama. Rodney Walkerley was commentator at Silverstone in those days and he vividly remembers the occasion: 'Raymond Sommer, a rich amateur from Paris and a noted pre-war driver, was at the wheel of the BRM and he was allowed to put in three practice laps during which the scream of the engine with its two-stage blowers, had the crowd dancing up and down. Then came the start of the trophy race, with the BRM occupying the rear position. When the flag fell the BRM leapt upwards a foot and maybe a foot forward before it sank back in a pool of oil.'

The drive-shaft had failed as Sommer let in the clutch and Britain's hopes of an exciting display from the BRM were punctured in a misery of anti-climax. One interesting sidelight to the debut of the BRMs at Silverstone: the first-aiders had to deal with several hundreds of extra cases. The noise was so great that many spectators had stuffed paper in their ears and could not get it out. There were always more casualties in the crowd than on the circuit at Silverstone!

There was perhaps even greater sensation and certainly more action from the BRMs the following year when they made their racing debut at Silverstone in the 1951 British Grand Prix. Again the cars arrived late for official practice and were obliged to start in the back row of the grid. Reg Parnell and Peter Walker were driving. A feature of that grid, incidentally, were the two A12 4.5 Ferraris and two 158 Alfas on the front row, which was then a unique sight. In practice neither Farina nor Fangio in the Alfas could equal the 100.65 mph of Gonzales in his Ferrari. In the race, again great drama centred on the BRMs. During the latter half of the race both cars got almost red hot in the cockpit, resulting from bad insulation, but both drivers with great courage kept driving hard in spite of being badly burned. Their shoes were almost burnt off, their hands were blistered. Walker was half conscious at the end and both he and Parnell needed medical attention. In spite of intense pain, Parnell passed Sanesi's Alfa to finish fifth and Walker was closing on Sanesi and finished seventh.

William Hartley talked to Reg Parnell after the race and reported in the *Sketch*: 'He was indeed a tired man, suffering almost without sign, the painful burns of leg and hand which must have made the 270 miles a ghastly experience. His determination to bring a measure of success to the BRM, no matter what personal suffering, places him high on any list of men of achievements and Peter Walker, enduring the same, is there too with honour.'

It was a sad baptism for the hopes of a potential British world beater. And little wonder that Reg Parnell, when asked by the BBC's commentator what he suggested BRM might do next, in terms of development, retorted: 'Ah suggest they burn t' bloody thing.' The BRM – derived from the British Motor Research Trust – had been seen as an exciting Formula 1 racing car potentially capable of breaking all existing European circuit records, a $1\frac{1}{2}$ litre, 16-cylinder giant developing 400 bhp. When Grand Prix racing was being held to Formula 2 rules in 1952 the cars were still not sorted out and at the end of that year they were put up for sale with all the equipment. Sir Alfred Owen bought them and the Owen Organisation raced them until the end of the 1955 season.

'An amusing aside to the failure of the BRM at this stage,' remembers Rob Walker, 'was the superb cartoon in the *Express* by Giles of grandma's little children looking into the radiator of the car as it was standing on the start line. As we know the BRM didn't move very far on that first appearance and the following day Giles came out with another cartoon showing a mechanic peering into the BRM and pulling one of grandma's little children out of the engine, and this was obviously what had gone wrong with it.'

Silverstone at this time was the scene of the greatest dramas and most of the action in British motor racing and the latest sensational failure of the much-ballyhooed BRMs had come only a few months after one of the most spectacular events in motor racing history. It was May 5, 1951, the day of the *Daily Express* Trophy meeting, to be run in the usual two heats and a final on the perimeter lap of 2.88 miles. Ferrari were absent, but Alfas sent four cars, driven by Farina, Fangio, Sanesi and Bonetto. There was excitement in the first heat when Parnell in Vandervell's 4.5 litre Ferrari unblown Thinwall Special passed Bonetto with ease and closed fast on Fangio. After leading by 15 secs, Fangio was only 3 secs ahead of Parnell at the end, the former lapping at 96.29 mph, with Parnell just 2 secs slower.

Then came the dramatic final, a race of 35 laps and 103 miles. The sky was black and as the grid formed up the rain came. It hailed. It thundered. The cars looked more like motor boats, drivers could not see and parts of the course became flooded. It was difficult to make out the cars, several of which stopped in the floods with their drivers revving hard to clear plugs. Reg Parnell had torn into the lead, with Duncan Hamilton's 4.5 Talbot a good second. The rest were nowhere. Fangio and Farina did what they could but it was hopeless. After six laps the race was abandoned because the timekeepers said they could no longer see the car numbers and observers round the track reported the floods dangerous at high speeds.

Commentator Rodney Walkerley was in his box above the pits and finish line and had a personal anxiety to contend with: 'The rain was pouring through the roof and soaking my lap chart. Then a message came to me that my brother Tom, in the steel tube scaffold box over at Stowe, had been struck by lightning. I called Tom anxiously on the open loudspeaker system. "Tom, are you all right," I enquired. "I'm told you've been struck by lightning."

"Oh, have I," he replied calmly... and the roar of laughter from the grandstand could be heard above the storm!'

When the stewards stopped the race they awarded the prize to Parnell and Walkerley announced the order as Parnell, Hamilton, Graham Whitehead in the ERA, and then Fangio in the Alfa. There was an argument because the official order had put Fangio ahead of Whitehead. 'Graham asked me who was right,' explained Rodney, 'and then put in a protest to the Stewards. I was a witness at the RAC tribunal and stated that I was certain the ERA was a couple of lengths ahead of the Alfa. However, the verdict was a tie for third place, Fangio and Whitehead.'

More than twenty years later Rodney Walkerley still considers he was right. 'I had a better view than anyone, being high up, and the judges of fact at the line could not see the car numbers as I could,' he claimed; then added: 'Besides, I was more familiar with the cars!'

In spite of what Rodney Walkerley says, however, the official records were to credit Fangio with shared third place . . . but the real victory of the day was scored by the weather and perhaps Fangio produced the most telling quote when he commented disdainfully: 'Only the English could race in weather like that.'

By this time the *Express* Trophy meeting was with justification receiving acclaim as the greatest speed event in the British motoring calendar. As Basil Cardew pointed out in the official programme: 'At no other track in the world can people see, in one day, these widely differing attractions: (1) A Grand Prix type of car event specially shortened to hold the spectators interest which often wearies in the endless laps of longer races. (2) A race confined to genuine production models, which afford the chance of watching a car of your choice matched in open competition with its rivals in engine size or in price. (3) The world's greatest exponents of the 500 cc movement gathered together in the newest and fastest half-litre cars. They will fight it out in a short and spectacular 15-lap race.'

The 500 cc race had originally been introduced into the *Express* race programme as a fascinating curtain-raiser, but within just four years it had become established as a major event in its own right. There were two main reasons for this. First, it had captured the support of not only some of the best drivers in Britain, but also those of France, Italy and other Continental countries, probably because 500 cc racing costs were much lower than the cost of racing bigger cars, and also because in relation to their size they were faster than most racing cars three times their size, giving a greater sensation of speed and thrills. The second reason the *Express* undoubtedly had for promoting these races was that British drivers and British cars had within just four years excelled in the event, and a patriotic win does much for domestic motoring in any country.

Similarly, the idea of a production car race first introduced in the *Express* event in 1949, had now been established as a sound idea, for the thrill of watching everyday cars you could see daily on the roads of Britain, fighting for the distinction of being fastest round Silverstone, held a special attraction all its own. Some measure of the popularity from a competitors point of view of these production car races can be gathered from the entries. For the two one-hour production car races of 1951 there were nearly 100, though only 60 could be admitted by the British Racing Drivers' Club. Among them were numerous factory-inspired teams.

Finally, of course, there was the supreme excitement and spectacle of the International Trophy race itself producing, as the programme of the day announced, 'the greatest galaxy of race drivers and cars ever assembled here'. Ever mindful of the need to encourage the individual in motor sport, the *Express* event of 1951 offered for the first time a special prize of £100 for the best placed privately-owned car, irrespective of the winner, and there was a £25 cheque for the "mechanics responsible for the spanner-nursing".

It was all a lavish undertaking for more than twenty years ago and only at Silverstone, through the energy and enterprise of the BRDC and the *Daily Express*, could such a feast of racing be seen. That this particular event should reach its peak in a deluge of rain only served to heighten the drama and sensation for which the circuit was now reputed.

For the RAC, however Silverstone continued to be something of an embarrassment. They were concerned about the criticism, however ill-informed it might have been, that they were trying to make great profits out of the Silverstone venture.

But most of all they were rightly conscious that the running of a race circuit was not part of their basic responsibility as the governing body of motor sport in Britain, and that they had only taken Silverstone in hand as a practical means of hauling Britain back into international motor racing, when otherwise the opportunity would certainly have been lost for ever. To be fair the RAC had never regarded their direct influence at Silverstone as anything other than a temporary expedient and it came as no surprise when they proposed to let the lease of Silverstone lapse at the end of 1951. For a time the fate of the now famous track seemed to be in the balance, but then the BRDC with great courage took over the lease from the RAC, a move which heralded a new and brilliant era in the life of Britain's premier circuit.

So RAC Chairman Wilfrid Andrews reported in July 1951: 'The lease of Silverstone will not be renewed after 1951.' He referred to the volume of work in other directions and then went on: 'It is obviously undesirable for a governing body itself to own a course and there is the question as to whether, in the present circumstances, it is wise to organise events which might be run by other specialist clubs with greater advantage to the sport as a whole.'

William Hartley probably expressed the attitude of the sport in general when he wrote: 'The RAC have done their share in finding it and setting it up, but it is not for them as the governing body of motor sport in Great Britain to act also as promoters.'

That happened in 1952, but before rushing ahead let us look in more detail at that important year of 1950 when Silverstone, after only two years, was honoured by being chosen as the venue for the first post-war Grand Prix d'Europe and became historic as the background to motor racing which was seen for the first time ever by a reigning British monarch.

4

Grand Prix d'Europe

Motor racing history was made at Silverstone on Saturday, May 13, 1950. The third post-war British Grand Prix was given European status, a distinction never before conferred on the United Kingdom, and the racing was seen by King George VI, the first time the reigning sovereign had attended a motor race in Great Britain. We are told that so enthusiastic did he become that when the police insisted he leave before the end to avoid the density of the departing crowd, he was visibly annoyed and withdrew only under protest.

Not that the racing that day was particularly thrilling. The Alfas started in line abreast at the front of the grid and led the race in line ahead all the way. Yet it was a wonderful spectacle and demonstration of modern Formula 1 cars in action with top drivers. The crowd, responding to the special circumstances of the occasion, loved it.

It was a memorable day for those who had led the Silverstone crusade. Within a mere two years, the fledgeling they had brought into the world was being honoured by Royalty and immortalised by the Federation Internationale de l'Automobile, the international controlling body for motor sport, who had never before given European status to a motor race outside Italy and France. What more could they want? Silverstone maintained its high-flying reputation and there was again a huge crowd to share its greatest triumph to date.

This was a motor race to make history long before the cars came to the starting line. Negotiations with Buckingham Palace concerning the proposed visit by Their Majesties had started months before in an atmosphere of secrecy, but by February the news was beginning to break with an accompanying build-up of expectancy and excitement, even with three months still to go to the great event.

The staging of any Grand Prix takes plenty of investment and the Grand Prix d'Europe could not be allowed to suffer for the want of adequate finance. The RAC's original budget for the day was £20,000, soon uplifted to almost £22,000 as the massive offensive to dress Silverstone in all its glory got underway. Starting money and expenses to competitors accounted for £4,600, with just £600 allocated to British entries. Prize money was pitched at £1,750, trophies valued at £150, while other expenditure including any necessary treatment of the track surface brought the cost to well over £18,000. The budget had been broadly based on the experience of the 1949 Grand Prix, when receipts had been £17,667. With the additional status of the Grand Prix d'Europe, plus the obvious draw of having Their Majesties present, the RAC reckoned receipts would reach £20,000, yielding a national profit of £2,000.

Although the gross profit from that day was in fact something over £12,000, the RAC Committee meeting of June 20, 1950, was given the salutary warning that this figure was subject to considerable reduction 'due to expenses incurred by the associate section of the club in carrying out the arrangements for the meeting'. Net profit as finally revealed represented a satisfactory result for what had been, after all, Britain's biggest day in motor racing. By today's standards, of course, the various figures quoted would be regarded as 'petty cash'.

The Royal party consisted of the King and Queen, with HRH Princess Margaret, and the Earl and Countess Mountbatten, the Earl attending in his capacity as President of the Royal Automobile Club. Among the many VIPs in attendance were the president, two vice-presidents and the secretary general of the FIA, together with official international representatives from Argentina, Belgium, Holland, Italy, Norway, Portugal, Sweden, Switzerland and the United States.

Special arrangements had been made consistent with the importance of the occasion and a royal box had been constructed in the main grandstand, the stands and pit at that time being sited on the short straight up from Abbey Curve to Woodcote. Subsidiary special enclosures had been constructed at various points on the circuit where the Royal party was able to watch the cars at close quarters.

Royal Silverstone was gay and colourful, its naturally stolid, bleak façade transformed with bunting, streamers and hundreds of colourful national flags, marquees, the blue and gold of the Royal box, where the Royal Standard billowed in the warm breeze, and the warm companionship of almost 150,000 enthusiastic spectators. Even the sky was blue, the sunshine warm and there was the green of spring all around.

The day promised everything and in terms of an occasion, justified itself completely. Once the 30,000 cars had been parked and the music of the splendidly turned-out Grenadier Guards band was being enjoyed from more than 120 loudspeakers placed at strategic intervals around the area, spectators had moments to reflect on their part in the making of post-war motor racing history.

Never before, they knew, had a European Grand Prix been raced in Britain. Never before had the reigning British monarch been present at a motor race. But also, for the first time, they were to see a public demonstration of the exciting BRM, in which rested so much of Britain's hopes for the future; a British driver, Reg Parnell, in the all-conquering Alfa Romeo, again for the first time; and the first appearance in a motor race in England of the legendary Juan Manuel Fangio. Only the absence of the Ferraris, which could have battled royally with the Alfas, and the predictable nature of the racing in the major event blemished this exceptional day, but then only slightly. The hero once again, as in that first historic Grand Prix of 1948, was the occasion rather than the racing.

It was a supreme day for Silverstone and for seven hours she unashamedly put her talent on view: the procession of official cars at 10.30, the first heat of the International 500 cc race at 11.00, the second half an hour later. Then, prior to the final, came the demonstration of the BRM, three laps of the circuit starting at midday. Tension and excitement built up perceptibly to the arrival of the Royal party, scheduled for 2 pm, followed by their drive round the course and their presence in the Royal stand. The scheduled 70 laps of the Grand Prix d'Europe, estimated to take $2\frac{1}{4}$ hours, was due to be flagged off from the grid standing start at 3 pm exactly.

This then was the pattern of the day as the 500 cc cars created breathless moments with their full throttle cornering and spectacular slides. The racing was close. Stirling Moss was outstanding in his heat in the Cooper JAP, where Peter Collins, who was to run him so close in the final, could do no better than fifth, some seven seconds slower.

It was absorbing to see the redoubtable Coopers under pressure for once from the Iota Triumphs, particularly the car driven by Wing Commander Aikens, who finished fourth in the heat some three seconds behind Moss. The gallant Wing Commander was commonly referred to as 'Knees up Mother Brown', due to the seating posture of a tall man in a small car.

Stirling Moss had been outstanding in his heat and was hotly tipped to pull off the race, as thirty cars lined up on the grid for the final. John Cooper took an immediate lead, with Moss and Parker almost tied to his tail. Lapping at 80 mph Moss took the lead on lap 2 with Aikens now in second position. These two thereafter carried the race, Aikens going forward on the sixth lap, Moss taking over on the seventh, Aikens pushing to the front once again on the eighth. Moss made a monumental effort towards the end, but it was Aikens in the Iota Triumph who won the race by about two lengths, with Peter Collins only narrowly beaten by a despairing Stirling Moss suffering from 'vehicle failure'.

'By one o'clock (as Richard Hough in *British Grand Prix* noted), the final of the 500 was over, the BRM had done its *circuits d'Honneur,* and the Royal Party was taking luncheon. The King and Queen did a tour of the circuit and then went down to the paddock, where they were introduced to the drivers by Earl Howe and spent some time in conversation with them. The King showed special interest in the BRM which was housed in a regal pavilion behind the pits. Finally they took their places in the blue and gold Royal Box above the starting area.'

Race commentator for the day was distinguished motoring journalist and authority Rodney Walkerley, who retains vivid memories of the occasion: 'The King greeted all the Grand Prix drivers who were drawn up in a line to shake hands and bow. I remember that Farina, very much a Communist or left-wing socialist, showed every sign of delight and bowed low. He was a stiff-necked chap and very bitter about the war, in which he fought as a tank captain in the Alamein battle.'

The Alfas were driven by Fangio, Farina, Fagioli (at 52 bald, grey and grizzled), and, as guest, Reg Parnell, who had never driven a 158 Alfa until practice. Among other famous drivers of the period taking their place on the grid were Bira in the four-cylinder LT Maserati, Gerard in the ERA, Rosier (Talbot), David Hampshire, de Graffenried and Belgian Johnny Claes, 33-year-old son of a rich family who also ran a dance band.

Once the flag was down, the day became Alfa's. Behra, with a promise which was all too quickly dispelled, rushed along with the four front-of-the-grid Alfas, but at the end of the first lap Farina, who had been fastest in practice at 93.85 mph, was already five seconds ahead. The order changed only at fuel stops. Fangio and Farina swopped places several times in the opening stages until Fangio, to the surprise of the crowds and doubtless to himself, lost it at Stowe on the soft tarmac. The Alfas, unchallenged, slowed down towards the end, the three cars in line ahead and with Parnell, third as ordered, giving little doubt that with authority he might be untroubled in outpacing Fagioli.

In the telling these many years later, it all sounds tame and processional, related only casually to the tensions, dramas and close combat that is said to represent all that is best in Grand Prix racing. Yet there was thrill and excitement enough in the stirring, relentless, majestic manner of the Alfas' total victory. As Richard Hough in *British Grand Prix* put it: 'Their steadiness on corners, their breathtaking acceleration, their top speed in the 150s on the short straights, made a spectacle unequalled in Britain since the war; and the invigorating roar, switching in timbre almost in unison as changes down to third were made (Parnell in the higher-axled car a shade later) was a musical delight alone worth attendance payment.'

The manner of the Alfas' performance cannot be overstated, for this outstanding victory was achieved in cars which had seen little basic change from the original design more than ten years before.

For those who prefer more obvious excitement, there was an incident or two worthy of note. Fangio, in an attempt to catch Farina, overdid it at Stowe, waltzing through the straw bales, an incident which forced his retirement with a broken connecting-rod on the next lap; and Parnell's car found unexpected opposition from an unsuspecting hare, which appreciably altered the shape of his radiator grille and lower cowling. And if you took your eyes off the leaders for a moment, there was plenty of battle going on further downfield, as Harrison and Gerard fought hard for sixth and seventh positions in their somewhat lumbering ERAs.

Farina, at 44 years of age, went on to become the World's champion Driver, being the first occasion on which the C.I.S. had allowed this title to dominate the results of the Formula 1 International Championship series. In gaining the world title Farina won the Silverstone race and the Italian and Swiss GPs, with fastest laps in the Belgian, British and Swiss events.

The presence of Their Majesties was never quite forgotten, even in the most exciting moments of the race, and reports suggested that they had enjoyed the afternoon immensely. After a tour of the circuit on arrival, they had watched the massed start of the Grand Prix before moving to the special Royal boxes by the circuit where they could see the action at closer range. Rodney Walkerley recalls that their driver for the afternoon was Harry Stanley of the RAC and reputedly one of the best dressed men in London. 'Afterwards,' says Rodney, 'Harry told me that the King, also very correctly dressed in a lounge suit and bowler hat, was quite cross at having to leave before the race was over. He delayed his departure until the Chief Constables of Bucks and Northants said they could not police the exit route if he did not leave.'

Rodney remembers that his commentary point was like a telephone box slung under the outer pier of the footbridge, a similar box on the opposite pier was occupied by the lap scorers for the official scoreboard, headed by Stanley Sedgwick. 'For some reason I think there was no second commentator at Stowe that day, nor a relief for me. I was in that box from about 9.30 until after 6 pm and the RAC forgot to send me even a sandwich or a drink all day.'

One of the most vivid memories of a most memorable day for Rodney and many others occurred early in the morning as the crowds were streaming to the circuit. The four Alfas, in a long and orderly convoy from Banbury and driven by mechanics, came past in illegal racing trim on a public road, and the crowd cheered wildly and blew horns in salute. 'It was a splendid sight,' remembers Rodney.

Silverstone's day of days had given everything it had promised and *Motor* offered unabashed credit with the comment: 'The RAC is to be congratulated on the manner in which commendable showmanship has been exercised on this gala occasion. Grand Prix racing on the Continent, where it was born, enjoys a status reflected in the ceremonial and the trappings which accompany it. At Silverstone, we had a Continental atmosphere overlaid by that typical Englishry which attends our more important open-air sporting occasions.'

So much history was written on that special day at Silverstone in 1950 that the announcement about the formation of a BRM Association to help with funds for the development of a Grand Prix car to challenge and beat the best the Continent could offer, and the advance news that it would make its first appearance in the BRDC *Daily Express* International Trophy meeting at Silverstone in just three months time, were relegated to items of comparatively minor importance.

So much of Britain's dearest hopes rested with the BRM and as Raymond Mays took it on three demonstration laps of the circuit at the Grand Prix d'Europe, it looked powerful, convincing and impressive, even though he kept it well within its potential. The disappointment was all the more bitter and frustrating, therefore, when at the International meeting the car which had suggested so much hope before Royalty in May, was to falter so badly three months later (again in front of Royalty as, for the second time within four months, Silverstone was honoured, this time by a visit from the Duke of Edinburgh).

Drama behind the scenes, as described in detail in Chapter 3, brought a place on the starting grid for the first time ever to the British dream, the BRM, after many frustrating and palpitating hours for those actively involved. They fought a painful and tense battle to have it ready in time, feared more than once that the odds were too great, finally triumphed in lining it up with the Alfas, Ferraris and Maseratis, but then suffered the torture and humiliation of its collapse when the eyes of 100,000 people were on it.

The round-the-clock labour which was hoped would banish the serious supercharging and carburation problems finally only partially succeeded, one of the two BRMs scheduled to appear being made ready and flown to nearby Bicester airfield as late as race morning itself. With Raymond Sommer at the wheel, the car sounded magnificent and looked a champion as it streaked round in practice so that a BRM sensation seemed not such a wild idea.

Disastrously, the car did not even reach the final, its ultimate ignomony exposed to all, as history has now recorded, in the second heat, which was won by Fangio.

It was during this second heat that the day's top dramas and incidents occurred. On lap 1 Johnny Claes in a 1948 Talbot moved fast into Abbey Curve and, to avoid a collision with the car ahead, streaked off the road, rammed the straw bales and had his path checked by a barrier against which he came to settle. Had there been no barrier, there is every chance he would have crashed into the timekeeper's box. It was a near thing.

So magnificent was Bob Gerard's drive in his ancient ERA that in the early laps he pushed through ahead of Ascari in the Ferrari Thinwall Special to take second place behind Fangio. Ascari retired on the next lap. By this time a fierce storm was lashing Silverstone, giving drivers a hard time in controlling their cars on the wet surface, and at this point Shawe-Taylor was travelling as fast as Fangio to take over second spot from Gerard. At the end it was Fangio, Shawe-Taylor and Gerard.

In the final of the International Trophy Race the Italians dominated, Farina and Fangio driving their Alfas into first and second places. Peter Whitehead in a Ferrari was third, but the surprise and excitement of the day for the partisan crowd was the performance of Cuthbert Harrison, Bob Gerard and Brian Shawe-Taylor in late-1930s vintage ERAs. Their performance was incredible. Harrison was never lower placed than fourth for the whole race and finished in that position, while Shawe-Taylor and Gerard fought excitingly for fifth position, Gerard moving adroitly ahead until, astonishingly, he ran out of road while in sight of the finish and had to retire, giving Shawe-Taylor fifth position, with Stirling Moss finishing in sixth place.

The attendance of the Duke of Edinburgh had of course brought the Silverstone flair for special organisation to the fore once more, though the visit was far less formal than had been the Royal visit a few months before. 'He wasn't able to get there for the start,' remembers Desmond Scannell. 'As I recall, he flew into an RAF airfield, then he travelled part of the way by jeep. We had a car waiting to bring him the rest of the journey to Silverstone and it was all timed so that he arrived between events.'

In spite of the BRM's failure, the Duke seemed to enjoy the racing and afterwards the BRDC received the following letter from Lieutenant Michael Parker, RN, Equerry in Waiting to his Royal Highness: 'Prince Philip has asked me to thank you for the most exciting and thrilling day he had with you on Saturday at Silverstone. He was extremely interested in everything he saw, despite the fact that the BRM did not compete. The thing that his Royal Highness appreciated more than anything else was the way in which you all so readily accepted the problem of his coming for a short time and made a considerable number of arrangements when you were extremely busy organising the races. Would you please convey his Royal Highness' thanks to Mike Couper for showing him around the course.'

This was the first race contact between the club and Prince Philip, though His Royal Highness had been guest of honour at the Club's 21st birthday celebrations in December 1948, making presentations to a number of distinguished members including John Cobb, who had only recently broken his own 1939 land speed record. After the Duke of Kent was tragically killed during the war it was to the Duke of Edinburgh that the club turned for a new President-in-Chief in its Silver Jubilee Year, an office which on March 27 1952 Prince Philip said gave him much pleasure to accept.

5

Silverstone in the Fifties

In the beginning Silverstone was an expedient, a make-shift until something better could be found. When the British Racing Drivers' Club took over the lease in 1952 the hard times had by no means been left behind. A king-size question mark still clouded its long-term future and for all its sensational role in the post-war revival of motor racing in Britain, there were those old-time purists who found it difficult still to accept a coverted airfield as a permanent home for motor racing. Brooklands and Donington remained for them the ideal, but the times were different and outlooks and values changing.

The long haul to total acceptance began when the BRDC took over the lease and it was through the Club's energies, skill and influence during the 1950s particularly, that the remaining cob-webs of doubt were swept aside. Towards the end of the decade victory had been won and Silverstone was solidly established as a fine racing circuit with an international reputation, an essential venue for all the best drivers and racing cars in the world.

Founded, like Silverstone, among the deeper traditions of the sport, the British Racing Drivers' Club was well placed to hoist Silverstone firmly to its feet. The Club had come into being in 1928 as a follow-up to the private dinner parties held from about 1926 by race enthusiast Dr J. D. Benjafield, who wanted a club for British racing drivers. At about the same time A. V. Ebblewhite, who was then the chief timekeeper at Brook-lands, was thinking of forming a similar club for Brooklands drivers. The two men got together and the BRDC was formed. It remains one of the world's most selective clubs.

The RAC having 'primed the pump' by establishing Silverstone, it was up to the BRDC to increase the flow and they set about the job with guts and spirit, backed by the considerable influence of the *Daily Express*. A new lay-out for the start/ finish area was completed for the International meeting of 1952, the pits and grandstand being shifted to just round Woodcote corner on a short straight, with the paddock occupying the run-way behind the pits. From the stand spectators now had a closer view of the cars cornering and they were also able to see work going on in the pits. The new circuit measured 2.87 miles, against the former 3 miles.

The Club's task was massive, their resources in all departments limited. But they enjoyed an abundance of enthusiasm, native skill and knowledge, and a happy knack of knowing where to go to get a good job done on the cheap. Desmond Scannell was Club secretary at the time and remembers the spirit of co-operation which prevailed: 'When we wanted to take over the circuit, I wrote to between 200 and 300 members in 1951 saying that I was putting their name down for an interest-free loan and every single member came up with something. From this source alone the Club was able to raise £7,500 and it was this initial sum which enabled us to provide such essentials as permanent toilets and to build the permanent pits re-located by Woodcote.'

It was all a great challenge. Contacts and influence were used unashamedly in an endless struggle to make ends meet. If a member knew somebody, who might know somebody who could do a special job at a knock-down price . . . well, that was the way much of the early work was done. For example, committee member Kenneth Evans was a qualified surveyor and therefore the obvious choice to produce the BRDCs plans for improvement; he was also given the job of getting them approved.

All contributions were warmly and eagerly accepted, among them a cheque for £2,000 from Harry Ferguson, a Land-Rover from the Rover Company, an ambulance from Jaguar cars, and from Mr E. J. Newton of Notwen Oils there came a 30 cwt truck suitable for conversion into a recovery vehicle.

The continued support from the *Express* was crucial and the flair and promotional skills of the paper brought added gaiety and a sense of occasion to the circuit on race days. There was the banner running along the pits and lots of flags and bunting to give a festive atmosphere. Tom Blackburn's personal influence was a great comfort and inspiration, and more than once he was called upon to solve a tricky problem. At one Grand Prix all the programmes had been printed and the entries cleared when the Club had a late call from Italy with the offer of a three-entrant team. This foreign competition would be a fine attraction at Silverstone and Scannell said as much to Blackburn. Tom went to the printers and spoke as a friend to the father of the chapel there, whom he had known for twenty years. 'Set up this bit of type for me, will you, as a personal favour?' And the programme came out with the big, late attraction suitably billed.

'He was interested in people,' remembers Desmond Scannell. 'He would arrive at the track at about 7.30 in the morning and go round asking about the staff and making sure that they had everything they needed. On one very wet occasion, he was surprised to find many officials ill-equipped for the weather, squelching around in ordinary shoes. He asked if they had wellington boots and was surprised to discover that many of them had not. His chauffeur was sent off and returned within the hour, having spent a hectic time buying up all the gumboots he could find in nearby Northampton.'

Silverstone drained the club of capital, for the investment required was enormous and entertainment tax was crippling. One meeting made a loss after a bill for entertainment tax of £17,000 had been paid! With limited cash available, there were generally problems of attracting star drivers and teams from abroad. Ferrari were big and knew their value. As their status in world motor racing increased, so did their price, and often there were arguments; but Silverstone was establishing itself by now and mostly the BRDC with skilful haggling had its own way.

During that first season under the direct control of the British Racing Drivers' Club Silverstone was well used, four major public meetings and sixteen club meetings being staged. The short circuit was also used for testing on numerous occasions. In addition the G.P. circuit was made available to Jaguar Cars Limited, Aston Martin Limited and BRM, emphasising the close and almost inseparable links between the circuit and the major factories almost from the beginning.

A perpetually delicate situation was the presence of the farm within the circuit, still being worked, which restricted racing to certain days and times in the week. The farmer was a sitting

tenant with a lease and he did not take kindly to his crops being
trampled down by race-going crowds. There were regular arguments after race meetings in which he claimed damage to his
crops and the Club was faced with the prospect of compensation.
It must have been a unique problem for a race circuit and was to
remain as such for eight years until the club was finally able to
take over the farm itself.

There was a big job to be done and not always time to take
too much notice of the opposition. By today's standards in our
highly commercialised show-business world, the people who took
the decisions in those early days may seem to have been somewhat amateurish in their approach, but they did what they did
in a spirit of very real determination that Britain must have a
proper racing circuit.

Silverstone reflected the changing pattern of racing in the
1950s. We have seen how in 1950 there was little to approach
the performances of the Alfas, and that in 1951 came the Ferrari
challenge with Gonzales coming home the winner in the British
Grand Prix, though in 1952 third place was taken by a new young
driver, Mike Hawthorn, at the wheel of a front engined Cooper
Bristol; and the promising Connaughts finished 4th, 5th, 9th and
16th. The British Grand Prix of 1951, however, was historic,
for it was the very first time the 1½-litre supercharged Alfa was
beaten by the new 4½-litre unsupercharged Ferrari – the beginning of the end for Alfa and the start of Ferraris important
reign. It was also the first time Ferrari had sent a full team to
this country – Ascari, Villoresi and Gonzales. The four Alfas
were driven by Fangio, Farini, Sanesi and Bonetto. It was a
dramatic race which ended with Ferrari in first and third positions, Alfa occupying second and fourth. Ferrari had end Alfas
outstanding run of successes which had spanned more than five
years. By the end of 1951 the Alfa 159 1½ litre supercharged
cars had reached the end of their potential after fourteen years
and were being well beaten by the Ferraris towards the end of the
season. Alfa Romeo, not unexpectedly, withdrew from Grand
Prix racing at the end of 1951 and with BRM, which again did
not start in the Formula 1 race at the early season Turin meeting,
showing little promise of being able to offer a serious challenge to
Ferrari, prospects for the 1952 season looked dull and uninterest-
ing, unless you were excited by the prospect of the 4½ litre

Ferraris cantering through each Grand Prix to win at their own pace.

Faced with this tedious prospect, the organising clubs decided without exception that the Grandes Epreuves of 1952 should be run under Formula 2. Though the challenge to the 2 litre Ferraris was still not strong – they eventually won twenty-one Grands Prix out of the twenty-two in which their works team was entered – the change brought in the 6-cylinder Gordinis and Maseratis, though the Gordini proved unreliable in Grand Prix racing during the year. Outside challenges came from the British Connaught and Cooper Bristol.

In that first year of BRDC reign, Silverstone maintained its exciting reputation for thrills, incidents and fast times. The off-track dramas and difficulties encountered by the Club were of little concern to the average race enthusiast, who continued to make regular pilgrimages to the Northamptonshire circuit. On the delegation by the RAC of its racing responsibility to the BRDC, the latter strengthened even further its successful links with the *Express* and in 1952 the combined organisation put on both the International Trophy event in May and the British Grand Prix in July.

The new circuit was in use for the first race in the International Trophy meeting and in the final the crowd thrilled to the performance of Lance Macklin in a 2 litre unblown Formula 2 HWM. Both he and Tony Rolt, also in an HWM two seconds behind, had beaten a blown 1500 Maserati and two blown 1500 Ferraris! Here too, perhaps for the first time, were positive indications of times to come for a fast-developing Stirling Moss won both the touring car (Jaguar Mark VII) and sports car (Jaguar XK 120C) events, as well as being first home in the five laps race of the champions, while in one of the Trophy race heats Mike Hawthorn won in a Cooper Bristol 2 litre.

In the Grand Prix, Ferrari dominated with the factory team of Ascari and Taruffi coming home first and second. The race was significant because Ascari held the lead from beginning to end, the first time in the history of the series that such a commanding display had been seen. He was a complete lap ahead of Taruffi at the end, the astonishing memory of the occasion being that for all the change to Formula 2, the speed had gone down only fractionally, by as little as 5 miles per hour. Mike Hawthorn

showed signs of things to come by racing home third in the
Cooper Bristol, after pushing up his overall speed at half
distance from 86.94 to 88.24 mph.

Against the sophistication of later years, racing in the fifties
was vigorous and in many ways unscientific. These were the
days when drivers sat high in open cockpits and you could see
them working as they controlled their machines on corners and
almost read their expressions as they flashed along the straights.
Silverstone captured the picture for the mass of British fans who
now looked to the circuit as the established home of British motor
racing.

With two major successful meetings in 1952, the best days of
Silverstone were perhaps yet to come for it was at the circuit that
justice was finally seen to be done; having contributed so much to
the establishment of motor racing since the war, it was Silverstone
which witnessed the ascendancy of Britain in Grand Prix racing.

Although the first few years of the 1950s were lean ones for
the old country, with the well established continental brigade
dominant still in their Ferraris and Maseratis, the halcyon days
of such international stars as Stirling Moss, Peter Collins and
Mike Hawthorn were fast approaching, and it was towards the
end of the decade that rip-roaring characters like Graham Hill
and Innes Ireland began to dominate. Once again Silverstone was
in the vanguard and Innes has told how, after coming out of the
army in 1955 and racing a little in '56 and '57, he went up to
Scotland and while there received a telephone call from David
Murray, of Ecurie Ecosse, asking him down to Silverstone to test
one or two cars. At first he refused, but then accepted and from
that moment, at Silverstone, the sensational career of the out-
spoken and volatile Ireland was on its way.

It was the Grand Prix of 1953 which brought a fleeting
glimpse of the approaching glory for Britain. While the total
command of Ascari in the Ferrari, as in 1952, was never in
dispute – and yet again at no time during the race did he occupy
any position other than the leading one – the youthful Mike
Hawthorn produced some scintillating and exciting driving, as a
member of the Ferrari team along with Villoresi and Farina. On
the second lap he drove the Ferrari into and out of a gigantic
skid at Woodcote to the astonishment and delight of the crowd.
In his book *On the Grid* Peter Garnier describes the incident as

one of the most breathtaking he has ever seen – 'at Silverstone
Mike Hawthorn came round Woodcote corner in a tremendous
slide, spun round, and took to the grass verge, coming to rest
facing the wrong way round. Without hesitation he banged the
Ferrari into first gear, swung it round and with tremendous
wheel spin on the soft grass, was away, back in the race. The
crowd cheered wildly and with great appreciation of his courage.'
Mike had entered the corner at a thunderous rate, and at about
100 miles per hour finished up cascading mud and turves over a
wide area.

By 1954 a strong Mercedes challenge had enlivened the Grand
Prix scene and their new, enormously hot 8-cylinder advanced
machines were seen in Britain for the first time at Silverstone.
It was the first time since the war that the Germans had brought
their cars to a British track. They had already dominated the
French Grand Prix that year with Fangio lapping at an incredible
124.31 miles per hour and there was keen anticipation among the
large crowd at Silverstone: but their new W196, featuring a
straight eight engine with desmodromic valves and fuel injection,
laid on its side in the frame, inboard-mounted brakes front and
rear, and streamlined body work, was not suited to Silverstone
and even in the hands of Fangio and Karl Kling could do
nothing.

The Mercedes, with wheels hidden by the body, were out of
their element at Silverstone and Fangio began hitting marker
tubs in his pursuit of Gonzales in the Ferrari. Moss (as was
reported at the time), 'had his Maserati up in the sharp end of
the fight for eighty laps and then the back axle failed when he
was in second place. Fangio could do no better than fourth and
Kling was outclassed.' Exceptional indeed in that 1954 British
Grand Prix was the fact that seven drivers who all tied for the
fastest lap. The race served as a salutory lesson for the Mercedes
Benz factory, who, let it be said, had arrived at Silverstone with
a touch of arrogance following their impressive victory at Rheims.

The occasion was the first and only time the W196 apppeared
at Silverstone. It was Ferrari yet again, this time with the might
of Gonzales (first) and Hawthorn (second), which shone to take
the day's honours. There was drama when Gonzales' new style
Ferrari, which he had driven to commanding success in his heat,
refused to start for the final. He had to take over the type 625

of Trintignant, which he drove to a comfortable victory. The Mercedes, it is interesting to recall, were unstreamlined for the German Grand Prix which followed and thereafter, depending on the character of the circuit, were raced with or without streamlining.

1954 was, of course, the first season of the seven year formula – 2½ litres unsupercharged – during which British cars were to emerge from obscurity to win the World's Championship of Manufacturers three times. In 1955 the BRDC arranged for the International Trophy Race to be fought out in a straightforward 60-lap event, forsaking the heats-and-final arrangement of previous Trophy races. This increased the impact and drama in an event which gave an English crowd its first opportunity to see the new Connaught at Silverstone. Jack Fairman was driving and did magnificently to keep it up in third place for more than half the race when mechanical trouble stopped his challenge. Perhaps the outstanding memory of the event was the fierce struggle in the early stages between Peter Collins and Roy Salvadori in 250F Maseratis, Peter handling the car superbly to win.

Gaining impetus from Silverstone's success, other race circuits had, by now, become established and were rightfully hopeful of recognition. It was no surprise therefore that the British Grand Prix, after being held at Silverstone for seven consecutive years, was allocated to Aintree for 1955, but it was back at Silverstone the following year, though by this time Mercedes had once more disappeared from racing, and Ferraris took the first two places.

Motor racing at Silverstone was by now such a major attraction that the BBC offered a three year contract for exclusive TV coverage and sound broadcasting rights, the sum paid to be reduced when the Grand Prix was not staged at the circuit. By later standards of course the figure was puny, but then it was a fair sum and acceptable to Silverstone against a counter bid from ITV.

Towards the end of 1955 came news of the first British victory in a Grand Prix since 1924, when Tony Brooks, driving the British Connaught, was first against continental opposition in the Syracuse Grand Prix. It was an auspicious occasion, for the last time a British car had been driven to a Grand Prix victory was back in 1924 with Segrave at the wheel of his Sunbeam in the Spanish GP.

With all roads leading to Silverstone for the 1956 International Trophy meeting Britain's status had soared high and there was evidence to suggest that at last Britain had Grand Prix cars capable of equalling and, with luck, beating the fastest models coming from the Continent.

The Connaught had already shown its teeth against strong foreign opposition; plenty was expected of Tony Vandervell's Vanwall Special, which Stirling Moss had already nominated as the best behaved car he had ever driven and which Harry Schell and Maurice Trintignant of France were listed to drive; and of course there was the rebellious and precocious BRM, which always seemed on the verge of great things.

Events, or at least some, fulfilled the promise. It was Stirling Moss who finally drove the winning Vanwall at 100.47 mph, lapping the entire field, while Connaughts collected second and third with Archie Scott-Brown and Desmond Titterington at the controls. It was a great and exciting occasion for British motor racing, and appropriate that it should happen at Silverstone, which was to reflect the achievement of total domination over foreign rivals of British racing cars and British drivers during the years 1957–1960.

So in 1956 there were strong hopes that at Silverstone we should at last see a British driver in a British car flash past the winning flag first in our own Grand Prix. Excitement was intense as the dream of more than a decade seemed set for realisation. Mike Hawthorn rocketed from the front line of the grid at electrifying speed with Tony Brooks the only other driver remotely in a challenging position, coming through from the third row of the grid in sensational style. At one delirious moment five British drivers held the first five places and for fifteen laps Mike Hawthorn and Tony Brooks led the field for BRM. Surely nothing could now rob Britain of absolute triumph, but then both Mike and Tony were forced to retire with mechanical trouble, allowing Ferraris to take the first two places. Fangio, with Mercedes now out of racing, was with Ferrari and he won by three miles.

The British Grand Prix which had promised so much and which for the early part of the race looked strongly set to produce that first all-British GP victory, ended in ruins and disillusionment. In human terms, the salvation was the miraculous escape of

Tony Brooks, involved in one of the most spectacular and sensational sights to be seen at Silverstone. It occurred at Abbey
Corner when Tony, the throttle on his 4-cylinder BRM jammed
open, was incapable of negotiating the bend. The car careered
off the road, somersaulted, throwing him clear, and almost
immediately burst into a raging inferno.

That great milestone of an all-British victory in a home Grand
Prix finally came in 1957, but ironically not at Silverstone. Rough
justice indeed, but by now this major International event was
sharing alternate homes at Aintree and Silverstone and it was at
Aintree in that momentous year of 1957 that the British Vanwall
and Britain's Stirling Moss came together to produce a moment of
glory for the old country in that first post-war British Grand
Prix victory by a British driver in a British car. The famous
Northampton circuit was to make sure of another memorable
occasion, however, for it was at Silverstone, after so many toiling
and frustrating years, that the all-British BRM was to emerge in
full colours, to take the first three places in the September
BRDC *Daily Express* Trophy meeting of 1957. Behra and Schell
(specially released by Maserati for the occasion) and Flockhart
were the drivers in a race which was generally acknowledged to
be a welcome turning point in the history and fortune of the
BRM.

It had been hoped to see Moss in the all-conquering Vanwall
at this Silverstone meeting and the speculation which centred
around the possibility of a Vanwall/BRM duel was particularly
interesting. BRM had withdrawn from both Pescara and Monza
in order to prepare their cars for the big Silverstone meeting, and
when it became known that Tony Vandervell did not propose
showing the Vanwall at the September meeting, the grapevine
soon generated its own reasons. Some suggested that Vandervell
feared the challenge from BRM which, according to Stirling
Moss in his book *A Turn at the Wheel* was a 'fatuous and quite
obviously partisan suggestion, as a quick look at the records of the
two marques would show'. Tony's declared reason for not competing was that he had built the Vanwall to compete with and
defeat the cars of Italy and Germany and that as the September
meeting had not drawn an official foreign entry, it was
pointless to run the Vanwall. He further declared that if the
BRM wished seriously to challenge the Vanwall there was

every opportunity for them to do so in Grand Prix events.

It all heightened interest and kept the talk going, but the really significant point was that now, in 1957, it was not too difficult to accept the situation of two British factories good naturedly fighting with one another for the role of top dog in International racing.

The Suez crises had brought a fuel shortage so the International meeting that year was pushed back to September, and BRM, admittedly against opposition which might certainly have been stronger, romped home with a triumphant one, two and three.

Silverstone was now bringing the British race fans what they had wanted for years and took its share in showing them an increasing crop of home-spun victories. By 1958 Britain no longer had need to hang its head. Vanwall, BRM, Cooper and Lotus — these were the new names in international motor racing, capable of taking on the best that the Continent could offer. Cooper achievements were secured of course while giving away something like 500 cc to the true Formula 1 $2\frac{1}{2}$ litre racing cars, and Colin Chapman, producing a Formula 2 car fitted with similar variations on the Coventry Climax theme, was also coming rapidly onto the motor racing scene.

The British promise for 1958 was exceptional, for the old country was virtually on top in Grand Prix racing for the first time since the first event was held back in 1906 and certainly since the inception of the drivers championship in 1950. The year started with outstanding victories with Stirling Moss winning the Argentine Grand Prix driving sportsman-owner Rob Walker's two-litre Cooper. At Monaco's gruelling Grand Prix only six cars out of the sixteen starters were able to finish, but four of them were British. In Holland Britain tore through the opposition. Moss in the Vanwall was first home, Schell (BRM) was second, Behra (BRM) fourth, Salvadori (Cooper) sixth, Allison (Lotus) eighth, Brabham and Trintignant in Coopers. In the European Grand Prix in Belgium Tony Brooks, no longer the unknown he had been before his Grand Prix triumph at Syracuse in 1955, raced to victory in his Vanwall.

The 1958 International Trophy race marked the tenth year of Silverstone as a race circuit with an entry list which reads like a Who's Who of the top racing drivers of the day — Jean Behra, Harry Schell, Masten Gregory, Wolfgang Seidel, Roy Salvadori,

C

Jack Brabham, Stirling Moss, Maurice Trintignant, Peter Collins, Giorgio Scarlatti, Joakim Bonnier, Ken Kavanagh, Bruce Halford, Geoff Richardson, Steve Ouvaroff, Graham Hill, Cliff Allison, Richard Gibson, Bob Gerard, Stuart Lewis-Evans, Jim Russell, Anthony Marsh, Ron Moore, Ian Burgess, Bruce McLaren, Tony Brooks, Dennis Taylor, Ivor Bueb, Henry Taylor and others. Some, alas, are no longer with us and many no longer racing, although they prosper in different or associated fields.

Lined up on the grid were exciting BRMs, Maseratis, Coopers, Ferraris, Lotuses and a lone Connaught. It was a glorious day and with such human and mechanical talent on test, it is not surprising that lap records were broken. Behra dented the Formula 1 best, moving his BRM round in 1 min 40 secs, a speed of 105.37 mph. The Formula 2 record (1500 cc of course in those days) and the sports car record both went over the 101 mph mark too, Cliff Allison (Lotus) registering 1 min 43.4 secs (101.91 mph) in the former and Masten Gregory lapping in a Lister-Jaguar at 1 min 44 secs, 101.32 mph. And in the formula 3 race – still 500 cc – Stuart Lewis-Evans reached 1 min 54.0 secs to lap at 92.43 mph. The major Trophy race was won at an average speed of over 101 mph by Peter Collins' Ferrari; Roy Salvadori was second with Masten Gregory third, both of whom also topped 101 mph average.

Collins was untroubled after Behra in the BRM had his goggles shattered while leading the race, after which the event was noteworthy more for Peter's driving skill than for its epic racing.

If anything demonstrated the phenomenal progress of British racing drivers it was the British Grand Prix of 1958, for as the grid formed up at Silverstone it was the first time ever that two British drivers – Moss and Hawthorn – were in contention for the World Championship, their display in the French Grand Prix putting them on level terms with one another with 23 points apiece. This was ideal fodder for the pre-race publicity and everyone made the most of it, much to the delight of competitors and public alike. As Stirling pointed out: 'The Hawthorn-Moss duel for championship honours began prior to Silverstone and was instituted for the purpose of getting more spectators to Silverstone for the Grand Prix. Naturally we both wished to win the Championship and the public found this extra element of competition intriguing; it was further heightened by our differing characters and physical appearances – Mike, tall and blonde and outwardly carefree; myself, small and dark, the more dedicated, serious type.'

Moss took an important psychological advantage in first practice, hurtling his Vanwall round in 1 min 39.4 secs. Hawthorn had to be content with third best at 1 min 42.25 secs, with Tony Brooks sandwiched between at 1 min 41.6 secs. After Hawthorn came Salvadori and Collins. Further practice the following day saw Stirling still out in front while Schell got the BRM round in 1 min 39.8 secs, with Hawthorn and Collins fractionally slower.

In the Grand Prix proper, as so often happens, it was all a different story, even though Moss had boosted his ego further at this point, having convincingly won the sports car event, leading from beginning to end. It was a sunny day and the atmosphere at the start of the big race was electric. Stirling Moss in the Vanwall had taken the race the previous year at Aintree, from three Ferraris and a Cooper, and his followers had another celebration well in their sights as they saw their hero lead off the line like a rocket, well ahead into the first right-hander at Copse; but their hopes were short lived. Peter Collins in the Ferrari went ahead at Maggotts and in an outstanding display of driving, led for the remainder of the race. Mike Hawthorn, also in a Ferrari, was second and went on to take the World Championship that year, with Stirling Moss runner up. Stirling Moss described it all like this: 'To my enormous surprise Peter Collins simply left me standing as I came out of Copse. There was nothing I could do about it but hang on as close as I could. Every lap Peter continued to pull away from me, although I was also opening up a gap between myself and Mike (Hawthorn), who was obviously very content to await developments.

'Schell was fourth in the BRM and the other two Vanwalls fifth and sixth. At ten laps Peter led me by seven seconds, but at twenty laps I had snatched back two of them and Lewis-Evans had moved up to fourth. Tony had dropped back to ninth. Salvadori in the 2.2 litre Cooper took Stuart for fourth place at the twenty-five lap mark and then I had it.'

Stirling was having a great dice with Harry Schell when it happened: 'A rod broke, and as I came out of Woodcote I did not bother to go into the pits, but drove straight into the paddock. I think I realised then that my chances for the Championship had gone. It was still a possibility, but at Silverstone the Vanwall *should* have been the fastest car, but undisputedly the Ferrari was, which was going to make things tough. With my car out, Peter and Mike relaxed a little and the race became a procession, although the crowd were enjoying the sight of Salvadori's Cooper in third place ahead of Stuart in the Vanwall, a position he held until the end. Peter toured home to win, with Mike in second place. Mike had fastest lap as well to bring his points to 30 in the Championship race.'

Peter's speed had averaged something over 102 mph and he had covered the 225 miles in just over 2 hours 9 minutes.

A keenly anticipated British victory was thus denied the crowd in Silverstone's Tenth Anniversary Grand Prix, the decisiveness of their defeat proving especially unpalatable though, as Stirling Moss pointed out, 'the increasing speed and reliability of the Coopers, still with the 2.2 litre Climax engines, was obviously a hopeful sign for the future.'

Tragically, Silverstone's hero of the day, Peter Collins, was to die in the very next race when he went off the road at the Nurburgring while attempting to overtake the leading Vanwall. Collins had been among the winners at Silverstone almost from the first and in formula 3 racing secured the all-comers 100 mile race there in 1949 and was third in the RAC 500 cc race in 1950. In 1955 he won the *Daily Express* trophy driving the Owen Maserati 250F, and became a Ferrari works driver in 1956.

In 1959 the single seater Aston Martin made its debut at Silverstone in the International Trophy race. Two cars were entered for Salvadori and Texan Carroll Shelby. Ranged against them were two BRMs (Moss and Ron Flockhart), Ferraris (Tony Brooks and Phil Hill), Coopers (Jack Brabham, Masten Gregory, Jim Russell, Bruce McLaren), Cooper-Maserati (Jack Fairman), and Lotuses (Graham Hill and American Pete Lovely).

The first Cooper victory in the British Grand Prix came in 1959 with Jack Brabham driving. He dominated the event at Silverstone the following year and went on to take the World title for the second time in two years with five consecutive Grand Prix victories.

Earlier in the year, in private practice, Harry Schell had

lapped the circuit in under 1 min 39 secs, knocking over a second off Behra's record, and if no one could match this in official practice (Schell wasn't there), Moss got round in 1 min 39.2 secs, Brooks equalled Behra's 1 min 40 secs and sharing the front row with these two and Jack Brabham's 2.5 litre Cooper was Salvadori's Aston Martin, with an equal time with Brabham of 1 min 40.4 secs.

Shortly before the start of the 150-mile race a helicopter landed beside the track and out stepped Juan Manuel Fangio, five times world champion. He toured the circuit in a Land-Rover and was then handed the flag to start the race. Brabham led from the start, was passed by Moss and retook the lead when the BRM's brakes failed. He went on to win at 102.73 mph and in second place was Roy Salvadori in the brand-new front-engined Aston Martin, Britain's latest Grand Prix contender. Salvadori had equalled the lap record too, although no one managed to better it. Flockhart's BRM was third, and in sixth place came Jim Russell to win the Formula 2 section of the race, in the process lapping at 101.91 mph to equal that lap record. The Formula 1 Aston Martins, in which great promise had been expressed in spite of their traditional design, never fulfilled our greatest hopes, in spite of this commendable performance and soon disappeared from the Silverstone scene.

For Silverstone, the 1950s were significant, revealing and auspicious. The circuit had advanced with pride and rough dignity to a maturity and seniority which by general consent at home and on the Continent made it the premier racing circuit in the British Isles. It had produced in abundance the thrills, spectacle, sensation, victory and failure of big-time international motor racing at its best, drawing inevitably by its reputation and status alone, the biggest names and the most exciting machines in the business. Furthermore, the 1950s carried Silverstone through many important landmarks.

First of all, of course, there was the acceptance by the British Racing Drivers' Club in 1952 of the lease of Silverstone relinquished by the RAC. This enabled the circuit to forge strongly into what was perhaps its period of most significant development. In 1956 a similar decision assured the continuation of control of Silverstone by the BRDC for a further seven years, carrying it forward into the more sophisticated era of major

Grand Prix and International racing of the 1960s.

It was also in the 1950s that Jimmy Brown accepted the offer to transfer from the RAC to continued employment at Silverstone with the BRDC, a personal decision for which Silverstone and the BRDC have had continued reason to be grateful, for in human terms Jimmy Brown's courage, tenacity, skill and sheer capacity to get things done have made up much of Silverstone's strength over the years.

His day of decision was a telling moment in the fortunes of the circuit, because of all the hundreds of enthusiasts who have been closely tied to the progress of Silverstone at various times, Jimmy alone has been there since its foundings in 1948 in a position of importance and authority.

In the early days Jimmy lived in Silverstone village, and the respect for him there must have done much to allay any fears which the coming of a motor racing circuit might have provoked among the locals. His Silverstone contemporaries claim him as a man of rare and remarkable talent.

Talk to any full-time official or part-time helper at Silverstone and Brown's name is certain to enter the conversation. He is greatly respected and his major contribution to the progress of Silverstone fully acknowledged by all who know him. Jimmy's genius lies in his organisational flair allied to a calm approach, a completely unflappable character, and a lot of resource and inventiveness.

Jimmy Brown was later appointed a director of Silverstone Circuits Ltd upon its creation in 1966, and today is Marketing Director of the whole BRDC/Silverstone group of Companies.

Towards the end of the 1950s Silverstone reached yet another important stage in its history, for the operational assistance of the *Daily Express* which the BRDC had first enjoyed at that initial Trophy meeting in 1949, and which was later consolidated into a five year plan on the part of the newspaper to give motor racing in Britain a secure organisational background, finally came to an end by joint consent. After five years, it had been originally felt, the BRDC ought to be in a position to take over the raceday organisation at Silverstone completely, but the task was so enormous that help from the *Express* was required, and willingly given, for a further five years. So the Trophy meeting on May 2, 1959, was the first to be staged by the BRDC without the operational help of the *Express*. After working with the newspaper for ten years and fifteen Silverstone meetings, the BRDC now had to stand on its own feet as regards cash control, programme selling and many other operational tasks previously undertaken by *Express* personnel.

The success of Brabham in the British Cooper seemed a fitting tribute to the occasion, and there is at any rate no record of any organisational disaster having occurred.

6

Silverstone Spectacular

The 1960s were rich in racing talent. They were the golden years of Jim Clark, Jackie Stewart, Bruce McLaren, Jack Brabham, Denny Hulme, John Surtees and many other legendary names including, of course, Stirling Moss, who disappointingly failed to reach the ultimate success he so much earned at Silverstone.

All came regularly to the former airfield to demonstrate their daring and skill in the British Grand Prix and the *Daily Express* Trophy races. The circuit was solidly established with an international reputation, regular visits there being a self-imposed yet happy obligation for both established names and emerging stars alike. The world over, there was no circuit able to improve on the galaxy of talent on show at Silverstone during a big race day and in 1965, for instance, at the 17th International Trophy Meeting, the usual big crowd thrilled to no fewer than four drivers who had all become World Champions. Among them was the great John Surtees, an exciting and respected world champion on motor bikes and in cars. John was a popular hero at Silverstone, for it was there that he made his Formula 1 debut in May 1960 and such was his outstanding ability that within just two months he was racing runner-up to Jack Brabham in the British Grand Prix. Four years later he was World Champion, after a running battle with Jim Clark.

Silverstone was privileged to see many clashes between these two exceptional drivers and when Jim moved ahead of John to win the British Grand Prix of 1963, it was Clark's fourth Grand Prix victory in a row, a remarkable achievement.

From the start Silverstone was recognised as a very fast circuit and the 100 mph average target had been reached during the late 1950s. By 1960 the sight of a car speeding round Silverstone at a lap speed of more than 100 mph was still thrilling, if no longer a novelty, and Innes Ireland won the International Trophy Meeting that year in a Lotus at an average of 108.82 mph.

The British Grand Prix of 1960 was won at Silverstone by Jack Brabham at an average of 108.69 mph, though Graham Hill had produced the fastest lap at 111.62 mph in the BRM. Contrast Brabham's time at Silverstone with, for instance, Aintree where, a year earlier, he had won the 1959 Grand Prix at 89.88 mph.

Silverstone, which had fought a lone heroic battle to bring Grand Prix racing back to Britain in the immediate post-war period, was no longer alone. Goodwood had been established at about the same time and Aintree, Oulton Park and Brands Hatch were by now also flourishing. It was in the mid-1950s that it was decided to share the British Grand Prix between Silverstone and Aintree, each hosting the event in alternate years, but a later move brought in Brands Hatch replacing Aintree, though Silverstone, as the traditional home of those early post-war Grands Prix, was of course retained.

It was also in 1960 that Graham Hill joined BRM and he so very nearly won the British Grand Prix that year at Silverstone in a race which closed an era in the sport, for it was the last British Classic to be run to the $2\frac{1}{2}$ litre formula which was to expire at the end of 1960 after six years. He was well in the lead with only a few laps to go when he spun off at Copse. Having raced well in practice, Graham had started on the front row of the grid, but he stalled on the line and got shunted up the rear by Tony Brooks. When he did eventually race away after a push start he was at the back of the field. So superb was Graham's racing on that day that he was in sixth position by the twentieth lap and going strongly: fourth on lap 30, second on lap 38. Jack Brabham, having a wonderful year, was in the lead and it took Graham seventeen more laps before he edged past Jack to lead the race.

Graham opened up a small margin, but then suffered from fading brakes. With Jack chasing hard, Graham encountered two tail-enders as he approached Copse. If he followed them into the bend they would slow him down and Jack would be delighted with the chance to close the gap. Graham decided to move in first, put his foot down hard, arrived a little too quickly, spun off and finished in the ditch.

Graham, for all his outstanding talent, has often been unlucky in the British Grand Prix though that day at Silverstone in 1960 he came exceptionally close to total victory. He reckoned for many years later that it was one of his finest races as well as being one of his biggest disappointments.

Graham has had his 'moments' at Silverstone and is remembered from 1967 when, during practice for the British Grand Prix, he lost a wheel. He was driving his Lotus down the pit approach road on the inside of Woodcote when it ran out of control and he crashed into the retaining wall. As Graham said at the time: 'Bits of Lotus flew all over the place and my car slithered to a stop in a cloud of steam and smoke, looking very sorry for itself. I just stepped out and recovered a wheel that was rolling nonchalantly across the road, to remove it from the path of the oncoming cars, and then I helped the marshals to drag the car off the road.'

The mystery was cleared up later when it was discovered that the bracket securing the bottom left rear radius rod had come adrift from the monocoque section. As Graham braked to enter the pit road, it detached itself, the back wheel spun off at an angle and the car steered itself round sharply.

Graham's ambitions for the race the following day seemed hopeless but Colin Chapman stubbornly refused to accept defeat. He marshalled all the mechanics he could find, flew them back to the Lotus works and the team laboured through the night. They virtually built a new car from scratch for Graham to race and in fact were still desperately working on it when the cars formed up on the grid. It was a tremendous act of courage by Chapman and an overwhelming demonstration of devotion and commitment by his team of experts. With a car which had never been race driven, Graham took on an impossible cause, but by lap 26 he was astonishingly in the lead. For something like thirty more laps, Graham Hill in the night-shift Lotus held grimly to that number 1 position. It began to seem that a miracle of miracles would be seen at Silverstone that day.

Fate would have been kinder had it shown its grim face earlier, but to raise hopes out of such improbability made the blow all

all the more bitter when it was eventually delivered, at about three quarter distance.

One moment Graham was driving superbly into Becketts, the next the car was out of control. Incredibly, he managed to regain control. He slowed down and drove dejectedly back to the pits. In motor racing you adopt a philosophy of acceptance of what has to be, but this was a moment to stretch that philosophy to the very limit. For it was discovered that, in the rush to get the car ready for racing, one of the bolts which held the rear suspension to the body hadn't been properly tightened; it loosened and fell off, dropping the top of the rear suspension down and the rear wheel going with it, at the same time being pushed in at a crazy angle.

Graham Hill epitomised the success of the British motor racing driver of the 1960s. The high gloss of massive sponsorship and commercialism which came with the 1970s was unknown and Graham was a great character with a fine humour and an individuality which fitted ideally into the performance loneliness of the racing driver. He has a fondness for Silverstone and has spent many hours there, testing cars in the bleak greyness of an exposed and almost deserted circuit as well as racing before many thousands of excited spectators on a long sunny afternoon.

It was at the end of the 1959 season that Hill joined BRM, whose problems were still manifold and at times, seemingly insurmountable. For three years Graham and BRM struggled together, but the breakthrough for which BRM had been seeking since those valiant days a decade before, were not far distant; and it was Graham who saw them finally to success, taking the World Championship in the BRM in 1962.

For all its comparatively short life, Silverstone was the most historic race circuit in Britain and in 1960 it recorded yet another piece of history by bringing the British Empire Trophy Meeting to the circuit for the first time. This event was first run in 1932 as a development to the 500 miler at Brooklands, then reckoned to be the fastest motor race in the world, for members of the British Racing Drivers' Club.

The British Empire Trophy Race was held for four years at Brooklands, four years at Donington Park, from 1947 to 1953 at Douglas, Isle of Man, and for the following six years at Oulton Park. In 1960 it went to the Club's home circuit at Silverstone for the very first time and was there again the following year.

This move demonstrated once again Silverstone's involvement with the grass roots of motor racing, even in the comparative sophistication of the 1960s, for the British Empire Trophy had always been a race for members of the BRDC, organised by them in accordance with their wishes, and as such has enabled many star drivers of the future to cut their teeth in the finest atmosphere and traditions of motor racing.

The 1960 programme was published with a cover which was an exact replica of the one used for the programme of the first race in the series at Brooklands in 1932. It showed two cars on the Brooklands banking, one recognisable as the 1½ litre Delage with Lord Howe driving. At Silverstone in October, 1960, Lord Howe was a steward and also at the time President of the BRDC. The earlier Brooklands race was won at 126 mph. The first British Empire Trophy race at Silverstone was for Formula Junior cars and thus was unlikely to be quite so rapid. And in any case, the day was one of pouring rain with puddles all round the circuit. It was left to Henry Taylor, in a Tyrrell Lotus which he had never driven on a wet track before, to put on a masterly display of wet-road car control to win a race which he dominated throughout. His speed was 80.78 mph. Peter Arundell was second, also in a Lotus-Ford, at 80.51 mph.

There was a change for the next year because between seasons the International Automobile Federation had changed the Grand Prix formula from 2½ litre cars to 1½ litres, a most inopportune switch at that time for Britain, which lacked an up-to-date engine of that capacity. Pressure from the leading British drivers brought second thoughts from the International Sporting Commission, who agreed to a parallel Formula permitting the then existing 2½ litre cars to remain in international competition. This was the Intercontinental Formula for cars with up to 3 litres and with no limitation of weight. Cars and drivers in fact were, on the face of it, indistinguishable from a regular Formula 1 line-up, and once again Silverstone saw the debut of a brand-new car – this time the revolutionary four-wheel-drive Ferguson: impressive in practice, it suffered gearbox trouble after only a couple of laps in the race.

For the second British Empire Trophy Race to be held at

Silverstone, a fine list of entries was assembled, including Jack Brabham, Bruce McLaren, Henry Taylor, Dan Gurney, Stirling Moss, Jim Clark, Innes Ireland, Tony Brooks, Graham Hill, John Surtees and Roy Salvadori. The event, with its foundings in the savage speed of the Brooklands 500 Miles Race, has always been a great speed spectacle and with such a star-studded field, and with cars like the enlarged Vanwall said to give on the bench an eye-opening 300 bhp, speeds were expected to be high. Rodney Walkerley reckoned before the event that the lap record of 111.86 mph, then standing to Innes Ireland would be bettered. Once again it was wet, and when it was wet in those days it took a lot to catch Stirling Moss. It took a lot to catch him in the dry too, but on a wet track he was masterly. He won by nearly half-a-minute in front of Graham Hill's BRM: race average speed was 104.58 mph, and Stirling made fastest lap too at 1 min 36.4 secs (109.31 mph). Innes breathed again as his record remained intact. Stirling of course was one of the all-time greats and it was an apt tribute to his skill and courage when someone said of him: 'Produce a car to go round a corner at 100 mph and Moss will get it round at 101. The rest of us make do with 99.'

During Silverstone's early days many people, as we have witnessed, doubted the practical possibilities of Tom Blackburn's unlikely concept of a result every hour, yet within a short time the circuit had created, through the BRDC and the *Daily Express,* a thoroughly new approach to motor racing with a unique atmosphere. Now, through the scintillating years of the 1960s, Silverstone mounted a lavish programme of top flight racing, its pattern of gloss, pace, flair and showmanship being imitated with success by circuits in other parts of Britain and abroad. As one report put it, referring to the 1965 International Trophy Meeting: 'Before the day is out we will have seen a possible total of about 3,000 laps of the circuit covered by the worlds' most indomitable drivers involving more than 10,000 miles of top-line racing.' Silverstone shone brightly and you would be hard pressed to find a more concentrated, varied and ambitious programme anywhere in the world.

The imitation by other circuits was flattering, and the finest possible tribute to the efficiency and enthusiasm of the marshals — especially the paddock and start-line marshals, whose job it was

– and still is – to encourage, persuade, cajole, bully and even compel if all else fails, the cars and drivers to the right place at the right time. Such programmes were fiercely demanding and it said much for the enthusiasm, devotion, character and steadfastness of the officials that the Silverstone programme was held as an example, despite the mountainous problems it produced.

By the 1960s Silverstone had become one of the premier circuits in the whole of Europe, its efficiency a by word among drivers and the envy of race organisers everywhere. Formulae changed, so did the makes of race-winning cars and their drivers; but the crowds continued to flock to Silverstone to witness motor racing's passing show.

Let us see if we can pick out more of the important and dramatic events of the period. It started tragically with the death, during practice for the 1960 International Trophy race, of Harry Schell. This was Silverstone at its most uncharitable and unrelenting, a cold wet Friday when it demanded the ultimate sacrifice. Almost certainly, a heavy downpour had changed driving conditions. Harry crashed at Abbey Curve, was thrown out and died instantly. The accident robbed racing of a great and colourful character. Harry never reached the really big time, but he was well liked and widely respected in the game and his death shocked and numbed Silverstone that week-end.

Shortly after, that rugged character Innes Ireland, in an attempt to shake himself out of the shock of Harry's death, took to the track and brought Silverstone within an ace of its second disaster. In an effort to master the wet conditions, Innes hit one of the puddles at Woodcote, overdid his steer-correction, and rocketed over a small barrier wall at the entrance to the paddock area, before finishing up by ramming a nearby embankment. The car was badly damaged, but Ireland was luckily not hurt.

About this time Silverstone crowds witnessed Formula Junior cars lapping the popular circuit at speeds in excess of 100 mph, speeds not so long before considered unobtainable with a $2\frac{1}{2}$ litre car, yet these were models carrying what was basically a production car engine of 1000 cc or a little more. The secret rested mainly in the Formula Junior cars exceptional grip on the corners, enabling them to maintain high lap speeds.

The brilliance of our designers and tuners was now beginning to be rewarded and the early 1960s were important because Silverstone demonstrated just how complete was the British domination of big-time racing. Back in 1949 Silverstone's first 'International' was won by Alberto Ascari in a Ferrari at 89.58 mph. Farina was second in a Maserati and the first four cars were all Italian. Fourteen years later, in the equivalent event of 1963, how far the pendulum had swung Britain's way was forcibly demonstrated by Jim Clark's magnificent win in a British Lotus at 108.12 mph. Bruce McLaren in a Cooper was second, with Trevor Taylor (Lotus) third and Innes Ireland (Lotus BRM) fourth – not an Italian driver nor an Italian car in sight.

The International Trophy meeting of 1962 was rather special in that it was the twenty-first international meeting held at Silverstone, counting the successful Grands Prix of the RAC which had been run for them by the BRDC: and it was that year too that Innes Ireland was somewhat surprisingly given a fully-prepared works Ferrari Formula 1 car while *not* a member of the Ferrari works team. Ferrari had not entered a works team for the *Express* meeting, and Innes was astonished to receive a telephone call from Enzo Ferrari inviting him to Italy. They discussed the possibility of Innes driving and arrangements were finalised. The Italian marque came to Silverstone with their customary flourish, the car arriving in a works transporter and fully supported by a team of mechanics and technicians.

It was also at Silverstone that the hell raising escapades of the high-spirited Ireland made him into something of a national as well as local folk hero, for his monumental and now celebrated spin in a two-year-old Lotus took place in the pits area right in front of the grandstand crowd and in full view of the television cameras. He hit a patch of oil which John Surtees' car had deposited and, as Innes said, 'my car simply took charge of itself'. It spun round and round, though eventually Innes got going so well that he reached a lap speed which was not bettered for the whole of the season – a remarkable feat.

Also in 1962 the great Jim Clark was showing them all the way home in the British Grand Prix, held that year at Aintree, in what was to be a prelude to his years of outstanding achievement at Silverstone and elsewhere. A year later, again in the British

Grand Prix, keen interest centred around a battle for second place between John Surtees in a Ferrari and Graham Hill in the BRM. The latter ran out of fuel on, of all things, the final lap, allowing the Ferrari to take second place to an unsurpassed Jim Clark in the Lotus. Hill managed third position for all his misfortune and BRMs also collected fourth and fifth positions.

By 1964 Jim Clark was heading what was generally recognised to be the most powerful Lotus team ever put in the field. He took Silverstone's British Grand Prix in 1965 and was at the peak of his form, heading the World Drivers Championship. Graham Hill was there at Silverstone with Clark, plus an outstanding newcomer called Jackie Stewart. Great excitement also centred around the first appearance that year at Silverstone of the 12-cylinder Hondas, with Americans Richie Ginther and Ronnie Bucknum at the controls. Against them were full teams from BRM, Lotus and Brabham, plus a mumber of private entrants like Rob Walker. Clark was at the circuit again two years later for the corresponding race to complete an impressive series of five British Grand Prix victories, though on this occasion he was hotly challenged by Denny Hulme, who recorded the fastest lap at 121.12 mph.

Silverstone dramatically demonstrated its position in the vanguard of British motor racing at this Grand Prix of 1967, for it presented the crowd with a number of important 'firsts': Dan Gurney, who earlier in the year had become the first American driver to win a Grand Prix with an American car; Jack Brabham, as the first world champion who was also the world's leading Constructor; the Lotus-Ford which, at the Dutch Grand Prix had become the first post-war British car to win a major Grand Prix on its racing debut; and it was the first time that year that all the principal Formula 1 contenders had gathered together for the same race. Silverstone magic indeed.

Around the mid-sixties that exciting newcomer Jackie Stewart was getting himself noticed and in 1965 registered his first Formula 1 win, driving a BRM to victory in the International Trophy race at Silverstone. John Surtees in a Ferrari ran him close after Jack Brabham looked set to take the honours, but he was forced out with engine problems and a determined Stewart kept a three second margin between himself and Surtees. Only four years later Jackie was being tipped to take the world cham-

pionship from Graham Hill and was coolly admitting to Basil
Cardew personal earnings between £50,000 and £100,000 a year;
progress indeed and dramatic proof of the changes which had
taken place in Grand Prix racing since Silverstone blazed the
trail twenty years before.

The *Express* International meeting of 1968 was notable for
the devastating success of New Zealanders Denny Hulme, Bruce
McLaren and Chris Amon, who took the first three places. Little
wonder everyone called it Anzac Day. Fourth was Belgian ace
Jacky Ickx and the best a British driver could do was fifth,
Piers Courage in the V12 BRM. It was the fastest road race
ever run up to that time in Britain and only seven of the fourteen
starters made it to the end.

The pace was hot from the grid, with Hulme pushing it hard
at 123.10 mph by lap 4. The five leaders were grouped tightly
together – Spence, McLaren, Rodriguez, Hill and Hulme. Ickx
and Amon were well in contention. A stone crashed into Denny
Hulme's goggles and he did well not to loose control, though he
forfeited lead position, dropping back to seventh.

Bonnier, whose BRM-powered McLaren was faltering, went
out at Maggotts and BRM's challenge suffered when Rodriguez
could not get through Becketts because of ignition trouble. Hill
was now challenging strongly and had reached third place. Spence
still led with McLaren second, harassed by Hill. As McLaren
went to the front, Hill followed and made a supreme effort,
but once again at Silverstone, victory eluded him. A split fuel
line slowed him down going into Abbey and he was lucky not
to be rammed by a hotly pursuing Mike Spence.

Hulme had fought back magnificently and on lap 14 moved
into second position. Five laps later he set up a new lap record
at 125.53 mph to snatch the lead from McLaren. Spence was
third and there were renewed hopes for BRM as he moved ahead
of McLaren to take second place.

Hulme, Spence and McLaren ... this was the position as they
hurtled around, lap after lap. Then Mike Spence went out at
Club Corner with mechanical trouble, allowing Chris Amon to
move up into third position. Soon he was challenging McLaren
in a grim fight for second place but, incredibly, Chris Amon's
goggles too were struck by a stone and he had to battle to keep
control. As he came past the pits he flung the broken goggles

out, adjusting the spare goggles with one hand while controlling the hurtling Ferrari with the other. Though Amon failed to make an impression on Hulme and McLaren, who finished the race ahead of him, he had the consolation of being fastest, giving this particular prestige of Silverstone to Ferrari.

Silverstone's normally exuberant atmosphere was strangely subdued for this 1968 meeting as motor racing the world over mourned the death only three weeks before of the great Jim Clark, as a result of a crash in a minor race at Hockenheim in Germany. Jim Clark had done much for Britain and was acknowledged as one of the greatest racing drivers of all time. His loss was pin-pointed again a short time after at the 1968 British Grand Prix, which he should have attended to receive the BRDC Gold Star for surpassing Fangio's record of 24 Grand Prix victories – Jim's twenty-fifth being in South Africa on New Year's day. He had been a familiar figure at Silverstone and, of course, the winner of the RAC Grand Prix the year before. Silverstone paid its respects with a silent tribute to his memory, a Scottish piper playing a lament.

It was a sad occasion and further gloom lurked just ahead for within a few days of his exciting display in the International Trophy race, Mike Spence lost his life at Indianapolis.

As Silverstone prepared for 1969, reflective moments acknowledge the inevitable passing of time. Early favourites had departed the racing scene for a quieter life. Others had sacrificed themselves for the sport. Of the circuit's first Trophy meeting stewards, only the Duke of Richmond and Sir Tom Blackburn survived. Lord Howe, who had guided the BRDC as president for 36 years and was himself a distinguished racing driver earlier in life, had died after guiding the club's activities through many difficult and changing times; he had lived to see British drivers and cars dominate the racing scene. Also departed were famous figures like Sir Algernon Guinness, John Cobb, Dr J. D. Benjafield and Lt Col Goldie Gardner, though it was gratifying to observe three of the original judges from that first meeting, the Marquis of Camden, Lord Essendon and T. A. S. O. Mathison, on duty again twenty years later. Silverstone, as the legendary centre of motor racing in Britain, owed much to the dedication and drive of such enthusiasts, a heritage nurtured and developed in the 1960s and later by the Hon Gerald Lascelles as President of the BRDC.

On the circuit at Silverstone, 1969 was heralded as the year of new shapes and four-wheel drive. With Matra and Honda temporarily out of racing, Matra to improve and lighten their all-French V12 and Honda ruefully to consider their failure to match their glories of motor cycle racing in the car world, much interest and excitement was directed to the Cosworth-designed and built Ford DFV Formula 1 engine which, in the South African Grand Prix in March 1969, had powered cars into the first six positions. BRM looked for a good season, having just signed John Surtees, and the fast-developing Jackie Stewart had emerged as the new golden boy of motor racing. At Silverstone's British Grand Prix that year the Cosworth V8 engine reportedly powered thirteen of the seventeen starters.

All British drivers had that particular urge to do well at Silverstone: as Jackie Stewart said: 'We all make a special effort to limber up to our peak in time for the British Grand Prix. Call it sentiment, if you like, but we get a hell of a kick when we do well in front of our own countrymen.'

At Silverstone in 1969 Stewart's performance in front of the home crowd must have pleased him enormously. He was the winner in a Matra Ford, averaged 127.25 mph and created a new lap record at 129.61 mph. The event was notable for the fierce battle between Jackie and Jochen Rindt in a Lotus 49B, the latter's challenge hardly enhanced when his aerofoil came adrift and on the last lap he suffered the final irony when he ran out of petrol and could only finish in fourth place behind Ickx and McLaren.

Aerofoils, to the consternation of many, had by this time changed the appearance of the racing car. They seemed to appear, quite suddenly, almost between seasons and to the accompaniment of much derision in some quarters. Many authorities, concerned for safety, gave the aerofoil a short life and looked reverently for days when a racing car would yet again look like a racing car with, as one critic put it, 'wheels at each corner, an engine at the back and a driver tucked in the middle somewhere' But, of course, times were changing . . .

If the early foreign successes at Silverstone provided the incentive and drive to British car designers and drivers to ensure that Britain was not left behind in motor racing, then it was the spectacle and sheer festival of the racing which inspired the crowds to return to Silverstone time and time again. From the beginning Silverstone searched for new and appropriate ways of bringing motor racing in all its forms, stimulating interest on all sides by its enterprise. It would have been easy to follow the latest fad or to adopt the newest gimmick, but Silverstone refused to acknowledge such a temptation existed. Everything it did was adult and mature, respecting the pure and idealistic traditions of motor racing. It was radical, yet responsible: at the same time progressive yet traditional.

As we have seen, an historic feature of Silverstone's early meetings was the introduction for the first time of 500 cc races and of a race confined to genuine production models. Later came International Sports Car races, those stirring 'David and Goliath' duels; special events; GT racing; and races for historic vehicles. It all happened at Silverstone and the claims subsequently made in the official programme of the circuit were by no means overstated. For instance, at the 13th British Grand Prix in 1960: 'The racing programme here today promises spectacle and excitement for all, with a rich and most interesting programme of varied events in which cars of every description will be competing against each other.' Silverstone developed the reputation for showcasing great festivals of speed, with diversified programmes and a rare talent for satisfying the needs of the public while providing a breeding ground for future champions. For instance, many of the youngsters who originally competed in the Formula 3 events had their sights set on world honours in Formula 1 racing. The 500 cc events were established out of an immediate post-war need for an economical form of motor racing and enjoyed phenomenal success nurturing at the same time, much talent which was later to make headlines in Grand Prix racing, Stirling Moss being perhaps the most outstanding example. The GT events were races specially arranged for a completely new breed of sports touring car developed largely in Italy – large, powerful, fast, yet comfortable, luxurious, expensive and often in saloon form.

Saloon car events became extremely popular and developed an importance and interest to challenge the standing of the main Formula 1 races on the programme. They had a special thrill and excitement and there was an undoubted fascination in watching for instance, a car of your choice matched in open competition with its rival in engine size or in price. There is little doubt that saloon car events did much to give the average enthusiast a grasp and understanding of motor racing.

The first production car race at Silverstone was of one hour duration over 25 laps and few departures from production-line models were allowed. Three times the number of entries possible for acceptance were received including many gladiatorial names like Morgan, Jowett, Lea Francis, and Aston Martin.

The outright winner, as Basil Cardew later reported, 'was among the big boys where the old $4\frac{1}{2}$ litre Lagondas fought it out with the $4\frac{1}{2}$ litre Allards and the $3\frac{1}{2}$ litre Jaguars. In those days the Jaguars were driven by Prince Bira, Leslie Johnson and Peter Walker. This race was won by Johnson averaging 82.80 mph with Peter Walker second'. While the original fascination was in seeing cars virtually identical with those driven on the open road, the passing of time brought keener competition and sophistication to these races, the models raced being tuned and coaxed to their very highest level of performance so that in later years the cars may have looked the same, but the performance was, of course, very much superior. In the hands of drivers like Mike Hawthorn, Stirling Moss, Graham Hill and others, including that exceptional saloon car driver Peter Harper, the skill in handling a car of this kind at high speeds could fully be appreciated by the average driver, who delighted to the fiercely competitive atmosphere inherent in this kind of racing. On the other hand, crowds can soon become disenchanted on the slightest suspicion that they are being cheated. The fun was that these were basically ordinary cars and while the crowds accepted that changes must be made from normal production models, any radical change aimed at pure performance would defeat the whole purpose of it, reducing it to only academic interest.

Scrutiny in this form of racing has always been keen so that the changes of the racing models from the average on-the-road car were always kept within the legitimate limits. Most modifications were brought in for important safety reasons because saloon cars were never really constructed with a view to racing round circuits at high speeds; modifications like the strengthening of certain vital parts of the body and chassis.

That these events were spectacular there is no doubt. In fact what many observers feel is still the most sensational incident ever to take place at Silverstone was in one of these supporting races and involved Peter Harper, then a works driver for Rootes. Peter had been off the road twice before at Silverstone, once when he hit a 'water hole' at 100 mph. His car aqua-planed, the steering wheel spinning in his hand. As he described in his book *Destination Monte:* 'I saw a panicked race marshal leap to safety as I careered over a grass verge and headed straight towards him. Nearby was a brick wall and I hit it at about 90 mph. The first impact, luckily, was at an angle of about 45 degrees. The car ricocheted and hit the wall a second time . . . head on! The seat collapsed; the front of the car was shattered. But all I got was a stiff neck.'

The other occasion Peter left the circuit was while travelling ahead of 100 mph through Woodcote. A half shaft snapped. He developed a gigantic broadside, slithering to a halt in front of the pits. Says Peter with that dry wit of his : 'This episode provided me with one of my more amusing distinctions for I am the only driver so far as I know to break the class lap record at Silverstone while passing the timekeeper on three wheels and almost broadside on.'

But Peter's most spectacular shunt was in 1963. As he described most graphically in his book : 'Paddy Hopkirk was coming through on the inside, got carried away, and caught me a resounding thump. I spun round and Christabel Carlisle, following in a Mini, caught me. As my car rolled it picked Christabel's up with it and when the dust had settled there was the Mini . . . perched on top of my car. My first thought after my car had stopped was to get out quickly in case anyone else hit me, and was I amazed to see Christabel's Mini hanging up there.'

In saloon car racing Jaguars were overall masters for many years and in 1960 for instance these 3.8 litre saloons faced competition from Ford Zephyrs. Down the scale it is interesting to see that Volvo were leading the challenge in the 1.6 litre class with competition from a 1.5 Riley and Sunbeam Rapiers, while keen interest was focused on the small class with Morris and Austin minis facing Auto Union and Saab entries. But in the years to follow, domination in all classes of saloon car racing changed. Jaguar, Sunbeam, MG, Daimler, Austin A40 and A35,

Volvo, these were the names to excite at Silverstone in the earlier days of saloon car racing. Jaguar's invincibility crumpled when American Ford moved in with their exciting 7-litre Galaxies, and later they introduced the Mustang. Mercedes contested with success the 3 litre section, followed by Ford Lotus Cortina and then came the BMW challenge. Mini Coopers were outstanding for a long time in the smaller class.

It must be admitted that initially saloon car racing was the poor relation of a Silverstone race day, but before long it developed its own personality and an enthusiastic following which gave it a prestige and standing all its own.

In 1973 saloon car racing again excited and thrilled the crowds at Silverstone, but now, at the GKN-*Daily Express* Silver Jubilee International Trophy meeting, it was the 7-litre Chevrolet Camaro, with Frank Gardner at the controls, which was expected to dominate and in so doing, perhaps reach a new saloon car record at 115 mph, though anything over 111 mph would have been good enough. Ford were there with a hot challenge, this time with the Capri, and BMW were also expected to run the Camaro close. In the 2 litre classification, Ford Escorts were virtually assured of success and it was the Escorts again to which most people looked for good chances in the 1001 to 1300 cc section. In the small class Chrysler Imps were expected to dominate.

Silverstone set the pattern for others to follow. It was the constructive thinking of the BRDC and the *Daily Express* which brought in the idea of Production Car races and when this was seen to be successful, Silverstone saw its development with its division into two events for sports models and tourers, events which were to become classics. When Grand Touring racing came in it was the same combined talents which introduced it to Silverstone.

The Historic Car Races brought out again many splendid cars which had rushed to glorious victory in days past, bringing a special fascination and a touch of nostalgia – models like the magnificent Bugatti which had previously been raced by Stuart Fothringham and Kay Petre at Brooklands, no less; or the Cooper-Bristol which first brought Mike Hawthorn to race recognition.

Such innovations were introduced before racing drivers had long hair, but gradually we were conscious of a developing infiltration as golden tresses sprouted from beneath crash helmets and, almost before we knew it, skilful girl drivers like Anita Taylor and Christabel Carlisle were hurtling their cars round Silverstone. It was yet another interest which Silverstone welcomed, for many of these girls had great courage and exceptional driving skill. Anita's talent was particularly outstanding and, while remaining so attractively feminine, she placed herself in open competition with men to such an extent that she became the only girl to that time to gain a place in the Ford works team.

The variety of racing has always been a feature of the Silverstone race gala, but never have the supporting races been used as a substitute for what most of the crowd get most excited about, Formula 1 racing, for this is where the fastest laps are recorded, the giants of the sport are seen and the glamour and thrills are to be found. The standing of the British Grand Prix and the International Trophy meetings are beyond question, providing tangible evidence of the importance of Silverstone for more than twenty years.

7

Race Day at the Circuit

When Silverstone first became a racing circuit there were no grandstands, fences, or facilities of any kind. It was a wilderness of derelict buildings. The major problems were basic ones; how to get the spectators in, for the only entrance was that used by RAF security when it had been an operational airfield; how to get them out again; where to park all the cars they came in; and how to find enough lavatories for their day-long comfort.

Jimmy Brown, who was Circuit Manager in those days, admits: 'We relied on faith, hope, charity, rope and posts' ... and certainly there was no blueprint to work from.

Nowadays it is very different. The organisation is smooth and sophisticated, well tested and efficient: and Silverstone now has more flushing lavatories than the local Water Board can provide water to flush, and produces more effluent than the local RDC can take away.

Putting on one of Silverstone's spectacular shows is a massive undertaking and needs a small army of approaching 1,000 experts and part-time helpers to see it through successfully. But for all the organisation which now tries to make a day at Silverstone smooth and enjoyable, the whole thing is still made possible, as it was at the very first meeting, only with the help of hundreds of voluntary helpers whose devotion is so great that they often miss the racing and most of the fun, because their duties are behind the scenes.

That is a lesson learned from the first meeting, for a competitor then criticised: 'Far too many of the officials formed crowds to watch the race and took French leave from their jobs, while it was not over easy to find a particular chief who could give the information one wanted as a competitor.' (Cynics may

say there are some race-organising Clubs of whose officials this
is still true.)

Staging a Silverstone race meeting is akin to mounting a
television spectacular. The preparation and organisation, which
the public never sees, is endless; there are dramas and crises
before the show goes on. And always, everything must be right
on the day.

Preparations for a major event, such as the International
Trophy meeting, begin 18 months ahead when the Marketing
Director of Silverstone, having conferred with the Clerks of the
Course of all major events, submits on their behalf to the RAC,
the governing body of motor sport in Britain, proposed dates for
the major meetings to be held at Silverstone. These dates, along
with applications from all the other circuits in the country, are
sorted by the RAC and forwarded to the Commission Sportive
Internationale as the international body, for their consideration.
The CSI will first allocate dates for the classic Grands Prix,
as these have absolute priority, and will then sift the remaining
applications, allocating all the other important events. The grow-
ing world-wide popularity of motor racing makes competition
for the key fixtures greater each year and the job of selection
and allocation, once easy and straightforward, is now arduous and
complicated.

Once Silverstone has its dates allocated, the serious work by
Club Secretaries concerned begins with the drawing up of the
set of rules governing each event – length and nature of the race,
types of cars eligible, opening and closing dates for entries and
many other important conditions which form the Supplementary
Regulations; the basic rules which govern the conduct of all
motoring events being included in the International Sporting
Code. The regulations are then distributed to prospective entrants
and negotiations opened with foreign teams it is hoped will compete.

Meantime, Silverstone itself prepares for the forthcoming season. Maintenance work at the circuit, improvements and developments, all have to be timed to dovetail neatly. There are
conferences with the many contractors whose services will be required, artists and publicity people plan their posters, programmes, windscreen stickers and overall advertising campaigns.
The small army of officials must be told and fully briefed. Grad-

ually the tempo increases, building up to intense activity during the week of the race and culminating in a crescendo of excitement on race day itself.

At those first post-war meetings the public, only too happy to see major motor racing back in Britain, expected little of the organisation. Silverstone's efficiency was therefore a bonus, setting a high standard for the future.

As motor racing became more professional the support grew larger and so did the problems. Among those on duty at the *Daily Express* International Trophy meeting of 1952 for instance, when the BRDC celebrated its 25th anniversary, were five stewards, fifteen race observers, three judges, thirty doctors, eight ambulances, four scrutineers and three assistant scrutineers.

Seven miles of wire connected 175 loudspeakers and there were twenty telephones on the circuit. The thousands of spectators started arriving (in thousands of cars) at 4.30 in the morning and sleeping accommodation on the circuit was provided for 400 essential staff to make sure they would be ready for duty on time. Grandstand seating was provided for 12,000 spectators and the stands in which they sat were constructed out of a quarter of a million feet of scaffolding. Fifty thousand programmes were bought, tens of thousands of sandwiches eaten, and after everybody had gone home it took four days to gather up the twenty lorry loads of debris left behind by the crowd.

These days it is an even bigger job. It takes over a week to clear up all the left-overs, and the number of officials and staff on duty during race days has risen to between 700 and 800.

Communication at a major meeting is now an organisation in itself. The circuit has a Press and Publicity Officer, a Press Office and four Commentators. Programmes include interesting background articles and features, photographs of drivers and plenty of statistics, in addition to full race information. Always they are comprehensive and, when commemorating some special event like the Silver Jubilee of the International Trophy in April 1973, beautifully designed and printed. Provision has to be made for television and radio coverage.

Support services, often unobtrusive, are always present and have been improved over the years to give increased safety protection, bringing the best possible aid swiftly to the scene in the case of accident. In 1968 Silverstone instituted its own Emergency Services or Incident Team, to be responsible for providing drivers for the circuit's Ambulances, crews for the Fire and Rescue Tenders, and trained Incident Marshals manning appliances every 100 yards around the circuit. These key personnel are all specially trained volunteers of the British Motor Racing Marshals Club and there is now a team on duty at every meeting held at the circuit, from the smallest club event to a full International race meeting. Silverstone's Fire tenders, presented by the *Daily Express*, are specially equipped and converted Land-Rovers which are ideal for crossing open ground on the shortest route to an incident. These vehicles, resplendent in their team colours of red and yellow, are fully equipped with the latest fire extinguishing equipment and are positioned around the circuit to form a close support echelon for the Incident Marshals.

Incident vehicles, presented to the circuit by Duckham Oils, Patrick Motors Group and the Tricentrol Car Group, are fully equipped with rescue gear. These, as Phil Morom, head of Silverstone Emergency Services Team points out, 'incorporate comprehensive cutting and jacking equipment of the very latest design along with a formidable array of small tools and certain medical equipment which enable the crews rapidly and safely to effect the release of any driver unfortunate enough to become trapped in a damaged car'.

Three miles of circuit take a lot of policing, for the team's declared objective is to have fully dealt with any emergency in twenty seconds. These special services are supplemented on occasions of major meetings by the Northampton Fire Service, and units of St John Ambulance personnel.

As the big day approaches Silverstone transforms from its routine activity of cars going 'privately' round the circuit on test, to continuous movement and action as officials start arriving to check on arrangements and the circuit itself prepares its welcome for tens of thousands of spectators. The build-up is gradual yet exhilarating, more perceptible as cars and drivers, with their team managers, officials and mechanics arrive for practice.

A novice to the motor racing scene could well be forgiven for feeling that Silverstone might have overstaffed itself for its big-time meetings. Are all those hundreds of officials *really* necessary? Witnessing just one Silverstone spectacular at close range would fully satisfy any doubts, so efficiently is everything worked and so extensive is the programme of events.

Take for example, the John Player Grand Prix of 1973. With so little time between races, and only a one-hour break for lunch, the organisation was well stretched to give what was virtually a non-stop three-day festival of speed, although Tony Salmon of the BRDC says 'it was peanuts compared to a routine National Championships Sunday Meeting when we handle ten practice sessions and ten races between 11.30 am and 6 pm in a single day'.

Consider also the millions of pounds worth of racing machinery concentrated at the circuit, and the abundance of racing talent in the vast and impressive list of entries for each event.

Nerve centre of the entire operation, however, as the crowds swarm into Silverstone and the cars line up on the grid, is Race Control, equipped with a battery of telephones and specialised equipment, including the Autowriter which enables instant written messages from Race Control to the Press office and the Dunlop TV Tower Press room. Silverstone was said to be the first British Circuit to install such equipment, for the British Grand Prix of 1967.

Ever present at Silverstone on the occasion of a big race is the compelling 'circus' atmosphere to thrill and excite the crowds. Not only are the most successful and colourful racing drivers present, to be sought and besieged by autograph hunters, but also the charisma peculiar to the big occasion, the trappings of a big-money international event including the influential team managers and technicians, journalists and photographers, commentators and telly men, entrants, mechanics, wives and girl friends, hangers-on, public relations folk with their assistants, and sponsors, with their merchandising schemes, special posters and publicity, and dolly girl glamour teams.

The Grand Prix brings its own special brand of authentic atmosphere, full of tradition, with the top drivers chasing points for the World Championship. Its status is assured simply by virtue of what it is, though Silverstone's way of staging a Grand Prix is still accepted as a model by organisers of important race meetings in many parts of the world. Particularly remarkable, however, is the way the International Trophy meeting quickly developed into an essential curtain-raiser to the Grand Prix season for all the major racing factories and drivers. Aside from the Grands Prix themselves, the International Trophy meeting is noted as one of the most important and significant events in the entire European calendar. Factories plan their development programmes so their latest models will be ready for Silverstone in May, where Formula 1 drivers measure themselves against the opposition as a basis for possible performance in the Grand Prix rounds which follow.

As *Daily Express* motoring correspondent David Benson observed: 'In twenty-five years Silverstone can claim a unique record of never having missed an International Trophy meeting, and in those twenty-five years every great name in post-war racing has driven there.'

Of course, the pattern of racing at Silverstone is no longer novel. What it does is no longer unique. Yet its authority and influence as one of the really great motor racing circuits in Europe remains beyond question and communicates itself never more readily than on race day.

The super-star drivers; the most elaborate, expensive and sophisticated machinery; the most skilful and devoted mechanics and support teams; the most knowledgeable and enthusiastic crowds – all find their way to Silverstone, drawn more than twenty-five years later by the kind of big-time racing spectacular which Silverstone itself invented.

8

Motor Cycle Racing

When John Cobb performed his lap of honour officially to open the Silverstone circuit in 1948, it was not coincidence that he was escorted by three champions of motor cycle racing. From the start, Silverstone has been closely linked with this specialised and spectacular branch of motor sport, and what in 1974 became the John Player Motor Cycle Grand Prix, organised by the ACU (Auto Cycle Union), is, by its title, now recognised as the most important mainland event in Britain.

For years Silverstone was the home of the famous Hutchinson 100, not only England's oldest road race meeting dating back to the epic days of Brooklands in 1925, but until its move away from Silverstone in 1965, also the fastest motor cycle road race in the country, the impressive Mellano Trophy going to the winner.

Up to the time the race moved on from Silverstone, only five men had won this coveted trophy more than once, among them Mike Hailwood, who later continued racing round Silverstone in cars, and Jim Redman, six times world motor cycle champion and now retired.

'The Hutch', as it is commonly known, is organised by the British Motor Cycle Racing Club, which celebrated its Diamond Jubilee in 1969. The first Hutchinson 100, so named because it was organised in conjunction with the Hutchinson Tyre Company whose Mr A. V. Mellano presented the challenge cup to the winner, was run over 100 miles of the famous Brooklands circuit in 1925. It occupies a proud place in the history of motor cycle racing and came to Silverstone for the first time in 1949.

Although the historic TT Races on the Isle of Man had been resumed almost immediately following the end of the war, on the mainland suitable race circuits were hard to find. Silverstone's opening satisfied a specific need and once it had secured the Hutchinson 100, with its background of stirring action and deep tradition, assumed a status second only to the TTs themselves.

Silverstones' open corners make it a fast circuit for motor bikes and all the top riders have raced there, among them the legendary Geoff Duke. Geoff was an immaculate rider of exceptional style, neat and controlled. His earlier championship days were during the incredible domination of the sport by Norton, when he won both the 350 cc and 500 cc world titles for the famous company in 1951, repeating his success in the 350 cc category the following year.

British bikes had little time left in the big league. They were soon to wilt under the storming power and speed of the giants from Italy, MV and Gilera. Duke signed for Gilera and in 1953, '54 and '55 brought them the world 500 cc championship. The multi-cylinder Gilera was a new breed of racing machine, immensely powerful down the straights, its double overhead camshaft engine (70 horsepower, 10,400 rpm), beautifully machined. It could be rebellious, but Duke's superb technique and understanding constrained its mercurial temperament.

In the early 1950s, while Geoff Duke was racing successfully round the world, a young and dedicated racer called John Surtees was struggling for a toehold in the high-speed world of motor cycle racing. His first race at Silverstone was in the early 1950s on a Triumph. He was going well, but came a cropper when the con-rod broke.

In 1954 John was challenging Geoff strongly, but finding the veteran hard to catch. They came together at Silverstone that year in the Hutchinson 100. Surtees was on a Norton and Duke on the mighty Gilera. Heavy rain and treacherous track conditions brought the stewards together and they decided to cut the length of the race by half. From the start Duke, Surtees, and Bob Keeler on a Norton, moved out from the rest and it seemed that nothing could prevent John from taking the race. He was ahead of Geoff on the Gilera by a quarter of a mile when the Norton died, victim of stripped bevel gears. Surtees put up the fastest lap at 78.08 mph, but Duke went on to win.

John Surtees finally beat Geoff Duke in a handicap race at Aintree in 1955. It was a hollow victory for Surtees, who badly

(*Above*) An aerial view of the Silverstone club circuit, showing Becketts Corner in the foreground and the club straight leading to Woodcote Corner and the pit area. (*Below*) Royal Silverstone. King George VI and Queen Elizabeth attended the British Grand Prix at Silverstone in 1950. They are pictured here with Countess Mountbatten (left) and Princess Margaret (extreme right)

(*Above*) The International Trophy race in May 1951 had to be abandoned after six laps owing to a flooded track. Reg Parnell, the eventual winner, is pictured here sending up waves of spray from his Thin Wall Special. (*Below*) Post-race fun at the 1953 British Grand Prix with, left to right, Stirling Moss, Alberto Ascari and Ken Wharton

(*Above*) Copse Corner on the first lap of the 1953 Grand Prix, with Ascari (5) and Fangio (23) leading the field. (*Below*) The start of the 1955 *Daily Express* Trophy meeting, with Mike Hawthorn (1) leading

Fangio, 1956

Innes Ireland

Jack Brabham

FOUR WELL-KNOWN FACES AT SILVERSTONE DURING THE 1960S

John Surtees

Jim Clark

(*Above*) The start of the 1961 International Trophy race, which was won by Stirling Moss. (*Below*) Moss's paddock transport at the same meeting

Start of the 1962 International Trophy race, showing from left to right on the front row: Graham Hill (BRM), Jim Clark (Lotus), John Surtees (Lola) and Richie Ginther (BRM)

The Mini demonstration at the 1962 International Trophy meeting when, as the flag dropped, the cars took off in reverse

The saloon car race at the 1963 International Trophy meeting: Peter Harper's Sunbeam Rapier spins at Becketts

The car begins to roll——Christabel Carlisle's Mini is unable to avoid it

The final stages of the roll—

—the Rapier comes to rest with the Mini perched on top of it

Bruce McLaren talks with Princess Margaret and Lord Snowdon at the
1963 International Trophy meeting

(*Above*) The raised pit road under construction in 1964. (*Below*) Jackie Stewart, winner of the 1965 International Trophy meeting in a BRM, at speed during the final lap

(*Above*) Motor cycle racing at Silverstone: Mike Hailwood leads. (*Below*) John Surtees (Ferrari) leads Graham Hill (BRM) through Copse during the 1965 International Trophy meeting

Graham Hill jumps from his wrecked Lotus at Woodcote after the car had hit the protective brick wall at the pits approach during practice for the 1967 British Grand Prix

(*Above*) Silverstone in the 1970s: the start of the 1972 *Daily Express* International Trophy race. (*Below*) Peter Revson (left) and Emerson Fittipaldi set equal fastest time on the first day of practice for the 1973 International Trophy race, and chose to split their winnings

Peter Revson at speed in his Yardley McLaren during the 1973 International Trophy meeting, in which he finished fourth. He won the British Grand Prix at the same circuit later that year
Peter Williams at the 1973 John Player International at Silverstone

Race preparations. Mechanics prepare Ronnie Peterson's John Player
Special in the paddock at the 1973 International Trophy meeting (*above*).
(*Below*) Emerson Fittipaldi in the pits during practice

Ronnie Peterson at speed

Who else but Jackie Stewart?

wanted to win on equal terms to establish his position. That distinction came later that same year at Silverstone in a breath-taking 'Hutch' meeting. Riding an NSU in the 250 cc event, Surtees looked set to take the Mellano trophy and held the lead for eighteen of the twenty laps, but the machine developed valve-gear trouble at Stowe and he had to retire.

Having beaten Bob McIntyre to take the 350 cc event, John lined up on the grid for the 500 cc championship race determined to beat Geoff Duke. First blood was to Surtees, with Duke some five places back, suffering from a dragging clutch. Gradually the trouble cleared and Duke showed his exceptional style. He moved up the field and with only five laps remaining, was sitting on Surtees' rear wheel. John admitted later that he was giving the Norton all he could, but was unable to unhitch Duke. Luck was with Surtees at the crucial stage. With just a lap or two remaining, Geoff struck a patch of oil coming out of Club Corner, faltered, and did not regain his composure. Surtees won by seven seconds.

This first victory by John Surtees over Geoff Duke, achieved at Silverstone, heralded a new era in motor cycle racing. The next year Surtees left the Norton team to join MV-Augusta, capturing the 500 cc and 350 cc world titles for them for three years running from 1958. John became a popular figure at Silverstone for many years and when he retired from motor cycle racing with seven world titles to his credit, he was to return regularly to the famous circuit to race cars and then, even later, as a motor car constructor and team manager.

It was the sight of Geoff Duke and John Surtees battling at Silverstone which provided the inspiration for a young lad from Luton who was himself later to become a world champion. Phil Read, Yamaha team ace of the 1960s and 70s, used to go to Silverstone with his father and there had his first glimpse of Geoff in action on the Gilera. In his book *Prince of Speed* Phil recalls: 'Riding home from the Hutch on the pillion of my father's machine I began counting the days when I could swap the old side-valve Matchless and get out on the road with something worth showing off.'

Gilera retired from world competition in 1957, their gleaming world-beating machines being stored under dust covers in the marque's Italian factory. There they remained until a remarkable stroke of inspiration and enterprise by Geoff Duke brought them out once more on to the race track ... and to Silverstone where they were seen once again for the first time in England in six years.

During that time the Italian MV had secured a stranglehold on the 500 cc world championship. Duke, by then retired from active racing, persuaded Gilera to release their 1957 world beaters. He believed they stood a good chance of breaking MVs monopoly of the 500 cc championship. He engaged brilliant Derek Minter and John Hartle and the race game buzzed with expectancy. To the motor cycle racing enthusiast of 1963 the big Gileras were a legend, their reappearance at Silverstone bringing glorious history throbbing back to life in king-size form.

In pre-Silverstone tests at Monza Minter hurtled the Gilera round within a fraction of John Surtees' all-out lap record of 116 mph. The battle was set. By this time Mike Hailwood was riding for MV and the prospect of a Hailwood/Minter duel would open up old rivalries from the days when both struggled for recognition at circuits like Snetterton, Castle Combe and Brands Hatch.

At Silverstone, unfortunately, Mike and the MV were absent, but the Gileras' performances were both powerful and impressive. It was the 31st Hutchinson 100 meeting. The weather was appalling, but the big Gileras had brought out more than 25,000 fans. Though Minter was an established star by this time, this Gilera victory was his first on a 500 cc machine to be recorded at Silverstone.

Sadly, the keenly anticipated Gilera challenge was not sustained. First Minter, to be replaced by Phil Read, and then Hartle, crashed and Minter squabbled with Duke. What had opened at Silverstone as a crusade of outstanding promise faded into dismal anti-climax and with the MV with Hailwood aboard racing ahead to take the world championship for the sixth time in as many years, an incredible record.

Derek's enduring memories of Silverstone are of trying to control the rebellious Gilera, which was always difficult to steer and on a fast circuit like Silverstone tested a rider's skill all the way round. Remembers Derek from those days: 'Although there were no marker points for braking for corners, which was

a problem, I enjoyed racing at Silverstone. It was very quick in
my day and work on the circuit has made it faster still.'

Motor cycling racing was at its most vivid during the 1960s
when the Japanese mounted a gigantic campaign aimed at world
classic domination. Spearheaded by the massive Honda assault
and strongly supported by team riders of Yamaha and Suzuki,
these incredible machines were seen many times at Silverstone,
tearing round the circuit with exceptional verve and flourish.

The circuit did much to promote motor cycle racing to a new
generation of racing fans brought up in a four-wheel world.
A 5-lap motor cycle demonstration race was arranged in 1964
featuring many of the biggest names of the day: Mike Hailwood, then three times world champion and holder of the world's
one hour record at 144.82 mph; Bob Anderson; Derek Minter,
holder of the Silverstone lap record; Chris Conn; Joe Dunphy
and John Cooper. It also brought to the circuit the special thrills
of sidecar racing. As a prelude to the Hutchinson meeting in
1965, eight members of the British Motor Cycle Racing Club
gave a demonstration during the lunch interval, showing the
special thrills of sidecar racing on the Grand Prix circuit. As
was mentioned at the time: 'The sight of 28 outfits weaving
and jockeying for the all important first place at Copse is worth
travelling a long way to see.'

The last Hutchinson 100 meeting to be held at Silverstone
was in August 1965. In October 1970 came the news that there
was every chance of big-time racing returning to Silverstone the
following year. A full-blooded international was planned by the
ACU, and at once riders began to make plans. Mike Hailwood
had clocked a lap at almost 102 mph during practice on a 500
MV and the lap record was held jointly by Derek Minter and
John Hartle at 100.74 on 500 Nortons, but these speeds were
expected to be smashed once big-time motor cycle racing returned
to Silverstone.

Mike Hailwood had been Silverstone's star in 1965 when,
in the *Daily Express* trophy race, he secured a brilliant hat-
trick on a 500 MV, 350 AJS and 654 BSA Lightning. On the
spectacular week-end of August 21/22 in 1971, when the top
motor cycle racers were once more at Silverstone, Hailwood was
back, this time to battle with the great Italian rider, Giacomo
Agostini, who was making his first appearance at the circuit.

Other big names down to race were John Cooper, Phil Read, Rodney Gould and Barry Sheene, the long-haired Londoner and the new glamour-boy of racing.

It was a sensational week-end. Every lap record was smashed, a record crowd for a motor cycle event at Silverstone was established as 27,000 spectators saw what *Motor Cycle News* described as 'the best race in Britain for years.'

Paul Smart added more than 4 mph to the Minter/Hartle lap record of 1961, rushing round at 104.95 mph, the track's fast corners ideal for his Triumph-3. Smart won the Formula 750 race at an average of 103.401 mph, with Tait and Pickrell second and third. Hailwood was fourth and Cooper fifth. Barry Sheene took the 125 cc event on a Suzuki and the 250 cc race on a Yamaha. The 350 cc and 500 cc races were won by Agostini, MVs golden boy.

It was the performance of Sheene in the 250 cc event which was the big thrill of an amazing day of racing. For most of the race five riders fought for the lead, which changed several times a lap, but towards the end Swiss veteran Gyula Marsovszky inched his Yamaha ahead. After 11 of the 15 laps race only four-fifths of a second separated the first four. Sheene tore round the bends and on the last lap hoisted the class lap record to 100.16 mph and said he took Woodcote for the last time 10 mph faster than he had done before to move ahead and win the race.

This was an historic occasion, for Silverstone saw the debut in Britain of Finland's Jarno Saarinen, who was to become the major sensation of the early 1970s.

It was a great triumph for Silverstone and new record laps were established in every department. The ACU who organised the meeting, Players who sponsored it, the *Daily Express* who supported it, and the circuit's management were all delighted with the result and international motor cycle racing at Silverstone was once again seen as a major annual event. The circuit's wide, fast corners lent themselves to close racing and the fans loved it.

John Player, quick to see the potential of motor cycle racing at Silverstone, seized the chance to sponsor another John Player International the following year and subsequently entered into a five-year agreement to continue their support.

In the meantime Jarno Saarinen had rocked the sport with devastating rides in many parts of the world. He returned to Silverstone in 1972 as the 250 cc world champion and a new-style hero. Before a crowd of 28,000 he rode a series of devastating rides, staggering the opposition and leaving the crowd wide-eyed and open-mouthed.

In the 350 cc event Jarno made a poor start, but was in third place at Woodcote on the first lap. He kept in touch with the leaders, content to stay with them until the last lap. As they began the final race round he thrust his Yamaha into the lead and rocketed into a record lap of 104.33 mph.

Jarno was on the circuit again for the 250 cc race, fighting it out with old adversaries Rod Gould and Phil Read. It was furious riding, all three on Yamahas exceeding the previous 350 cc record! It was close, but Saarinen held out from Gould. Already a sensation with the Silverstone crowd, Jarno left his most breathtaking performance for the 15 laps all-comers race. On the 350 cc Yamaha he outpaced the 750 cc machines, taking the outright lap record to almost 107 mph. In theory he could be given little chance as he lined up with the bigger machines, but he moved off well and took the lead on the first corner. No one could catch him. In winning Silverstone at record speed Jarno Saarinen, by then dubbed the fantastic Finn, became the fastest motor cycle racer on Britain's circuits.

Big plans for the 1973 John Player meeting at Silverstone matched the occasion, for this was the track's 25th anniversary year and the event, held on August 11/12, introduced the new FIM Formula 750 championship to Britain.

Silverstone's sensation of the previous year was tragically not present. Saarinen, who was said to be more exciting than Hailwood, died at Monza in May 1973 in a 15-machine 120 mph pile-up which stunned the motor cycle racing world.

Jarno, however, had left a legacy of outstanding riding at Silverstone which the famous circuit set out to justify. Everything pointed to a sensational two days of racing in some of the hottest two-wheel action ever seen in Britain. Phil Read would be making his first British appearance since becoming world 500 cc champion, and sidecar ace Chris Vincent was to make his first outing of the season in one of the two 1000 cc three wheeler events, and all the major stars were due to be there.

Nine works bikes clashed in Silverstone's two 20-lap legs of the new FIM Formula 750 championship.

Star of the big 750 battle was Paul Smart, in brilliant form on his Suzuki. In Britain's first ever F750 FIM championship round, he won the first leg, crushing challenges from Yvon du Hamel, Barry Sheene, Jack Findlay, Peter Williams and John Dodds. The second leg turned out to be Silverstone's fastest ever motor cycle race, with Williams leading from the start. After four laps Williams was still in the lead, followed by Smart, the latter closing the gap with a new lap record. On the 19th lap of the 20-lap race, Smart nudged into the lead at Copse and as the crowd watched for Williams to respond all they saw was Peter's machine splutter and fade with electrical problems. Overall, Smart won from Findlay, Dodds and Sheene. In the 500 cc race Phil Read smashed his own 1972 record with a powerful lap of 105.37 mph, winning the encounter from Barry Sheene with Agostini in third place.

This fabulous meeting, played out in brilliant sunshine before a 45,000 crowd which made 1971's 27,000 seem like a sample, really set the seal upon Silverstone's status as the home not only of British motor racing but of motor cycle racing too. All that remained to be achieved was the accolade of a British Grand Prix held on a mainland British circuit of proven suitability for such an occasion, and this – as these words go into print – we now know would happen in 1974.

9

Hanging by a Thread

Like all great and enduring characters Silverstone has repeatedly shown an outstanding capacity for survival. Time and again its existence as a motor racing circuit has been in doubt, but always it withstood the crisis and revived, invigorated and strengthened in wind and character by the experience.

Its birth was traumatic, breached in a confused atmosphere of criticism, apathy and ridicule. How many times in those early years the sheer size of the task ahead brought Silverstone to its knees is anybody's guess. More obviously threatening was the constant vulnerability of its bank balance, repeatedly emaciated by the demands of entertainment tax. Yet always when the circuit began to falter, for whatever reason, disciples were close at hand; the RAC, whose faith sometimes wavered but never collapsed; the BRDC, who foresaw Silverstone's great future and became its long-term saviour; and the *Daily Express* whose unfailing support in the early days was beyond price.

The huge success of the first post-war meeting in 1948 ought to have secured Silverstone's future. Alas, the track shuffled uneasily from one short-term lease to another, stifled by tedious and long-winded contact with various ministries and inhibited by the self-doubts of the RAC itself, for it was never very seriously considered that they should be responsible for Silverstone indefinitely, however tempting the idea. RAC meetings held during this time tell their own story: *July 1949* – Chairman Wilfrid Andrews explained that the club would soon have to decide as to the continuance of the lease of the Silverstone circuit from the Air Ministry on a long-term basis. After reminding the committee of the reasons which prompted the club to obtain the use of the track in the first place (to assist in the reorganisation of motor sport following the war years) he expressed the opinion that careful thought would have to be given by the club before committing itself to any future policy in this regard. He referred to the considerable expense borne by the club, not only with regard to Silverstone but in the reorganisation of the Competitions Department for the improvement of its service to motor sport, and also to certain criticisms of those efforts and misapprehension concerning the monetary gains accruing to the club out of its lease of Silverstone. The chairman expressed the view that before a final decision was taken for continuance of the lease, the views of the Competitions Department, also of the executive committee of the club, should be sought in the light of past experience and with due regard to the terms set by the Air Ministry for a long term lease. It was agreed that Colonel Barnes, manager of the Competitions Department, be asked to press enquiries via the Air Ministry.

August 1949 – Chairman Wilfrid Andrews explained that arising out of correspondence with the Air Ministry regarding a possible long-term lease of Silverstone circuit, it had been established that control of the land was shortly to be relinquished by the Air Ministry in favour of the Ministry of Agriculture, from whom it was probable that a further lease for twelve months would be obtainable. The chairman agreed that an extension of the lease or a new lease upon these same terms be obtained if possible.

October 1949 – It was explained that, to date, no definite decision had been reached concerning a long-term lease of Silverstone circuit and that the club had not heard definitely on the matter from the Ministry as regards lease of the circuit for 1950. After very full discussion in which details of receipts and expenses were given, the chairman proposed and the committee agreed that a statement on the following lines be made: 'The club recognises itself as responsible for the conduct of motor sport in this country and while it does not feel justified in making a profit from the conduct or promotion of motor sporting events, it nevertheless feels that it has the right to reimburse itself for the costs incurred in this work. The club at present has no long-term contract in respect of Silverstone circuit and therefore its liabilities in this connection are unknown. If and when, however, such contract has been negotiated and subject to such reimbursement as is mentioned above, the club will hold in trust for the sport the balance of any monies received from such sources.'

December 1949 – A letter from the Ministry gave agreement that for the year 1950 the rental for Silverstone should be £900 and that beyond that date, no decision had been reached. With regard to the conditions of lease for 1950, while the Ministry accepted the points raised at the conferences including releasing the club from liability for upkeep of the track or runways excepting for necessary RAC requirements on November 3, details of the terms of the formal agreement had not so far been determined, but that information concerning this aspect of the matter would be sent to the club at an early date. A possibility was referred to that a development charge might be made upon the property by reason of the alteration of the character of its use and it was pointed out that no such charge would be made if such altered use was of no greater duration than twenty-eight days in one year. It was reported that the subject of alteration of use was now under consideration by Parliament. It was proposed to lease the circuit for the year 1950 only, at a rental of £900 plus rates, estimated at £450 and that by March 1950, it was anticipated that a decision would be possible concerning a lease of longer duration, bearing in mind the Festival of Britain when the club's contingent liabilities would be known.

March 1950 – The chairman reminded the committee of the necessity for a decision concerning the lease of Silverstone circuit as to whether the present lease should be extended to cover 1951 and possible future years or whether it should not be renewed on expiry of the present one year lease. He reminded the committee of certain advantages accruing to the club by reason of the lease of the track and of certain events which had in the past been run there.

May 1950 – It was reported that there was still no news regarding the rental to be charged for 1951, though the Ministry had been pressed on the matter. The delay, in the opinion of the solicitor, might have been due to the fact that they were awaiting information concerning the financial result of the Grand Prix event on May 13. A considerable discussion ensued as to the future plans when each member present expressed his personal views. The whole question however was deferred until the next meeting when it was hoped further information would be available.

July 1950 – The Chairman reported that the club had received a letter from the Ministry expressing willingness to renew the lease of Silverstone for 1951 on terms similar, and the same rental, £900, as during 1950. He advised the committee of the urgency of the decision in the matter and reminded them that a further meeting had been suggested which Lord Brabazon would be able to attend and to which it was proposed to invite Lord Howe and Colonel Barnes. In the absence abroad on duty of Colonel Barnes and of his own movements, it had been impossible so far to arrange a meeting, but he suggested in view of the club's position in the world of motor sport and its responsibility to other motoring clubs, that the lease of Silverstone for 1951 be agreed, but that no decision be come to at the moment as regards the promotion by the club of the Grand Prix event. After considerable discussion, the committee agreed to adopt the suggestion to lease the track for 1951, it being understood that this entailed no commitment as regards the organisation of a Grand Prix race on the track by the RAC itself. (Towards the end of 1950 there appears to be quite a lot of discussion concerning the relationship of the RAC with motor sport and, in fact, it had been agreed earlier that an adhoc sub-committee be set up to consider this particular problem.)

November 1951 – 'Lord Howe reported on the recent meeting with Mr Blackburn and other representatives of the *Daily Express*. The meeting had been most amicable and Mr Blackburn subsequently informed the secretary that the *Daily Express* would sponsor a meeting at Silverstone in each of the next four years. Lord Howe gave the committee some details of the *Daily Express* proposal to form a trust for the benefit of motor sport. Mr Erskine dealt with the draft heads of terms which had been received from Mr Cartwright, the Land Commissioner for Bucks. He said the first problem would be to deal with the requirements of the Town and Country Planning Act. In this connection his advice to the committee, which of course was gratefully accepted, was to go to the Northants and Bucks County Councils in the hope that they would agree to waive the necessity of applying for planning permission.'

These short extracts suggest something of the continuing

struggle necessary to keep the Silverstone dream alive and the tenuous state of the track's existence. The RAC fought an inner struggle as to whether or not it was doing the right thing; it battled against the slow tide of officialdom; it withstood well-meaning criticism from motor sport enthusiasts that it was unfairly making money out of Silverstone and that it was no part of the RACs responsibility to organise and promote motor racing in Britain.

Over four long years the struggle continued, but then came what on paper was the biggest potential threat of all to Silverstone's future. The RAC relinquished their lease of the track and William Hartley in the *Sketch* expressed some widely held fears when in August 1951 he wrote: 'No one will pretend that Silverstone is the ideal venue for major motor racing events in this country. The wide open spaces, inseparable from a converted aerodrome, provide little variety of corner and, important from the driver's point of view, almost no land marks to help with split second braking points. But many people, both those directly involved in motor sport and those who limit their interest to spectating, will feel regret if this season should be the end of Silverstone. It has filled very well the essential need for a racing circuit in the post-war surge of enthusiasm and the appreciation of that need that led the RAC Competitions Committee and in particular Earl Howe and Colonel Stanley Barnes to seek out a circuit has had a just reward. Unless the pre-war circuit of Donington Park or a similar type of circuit can be found and put into use, it would be a serious setback for motor racing in this country if none of the clubs or other bodies see their way clear to taking over the lease of Silverstone when the RAC let theirs lapse at the end of the season. Perhaps we might hope that in view of the motor industry's major part in overseas trade, the Government departments concerned will make the undertaking less formidable. Let us hope that news of a renewal of the Silverstone lease will reach us soon, as short of returning to Donington Park, British motoring needs it.'

In 1952 the British Racing Drivers' Club celebrated its Silver Jubilee with the news that the Duke of Edinburgh had agreed to become the club's President-in-Chief and that they had decided to take over the lease of Silverstone from the RAC. As Desmond Scannell said: 'No one else was in a position, or was prepared, to take it on. It was an enormous undertaking.'

The struggles which faced the club in their efforts to trans-
form the wilderness of this wartime airfield into a permanent
home for international racing are described in detail elsewhere
in this book by some of those who were personally involved or
who witnessed it at first hand, and it would be pointless to go
over the ground again. It should be said, however, that the days
of threats and doubts to Silverstone's continued existence were
by no means over, its difficulties continuing intermittently until
as late as 1970.

The priority at the start had been for a longer lease to give the
circuit more security. Ultimately, it was felt by the BRDC, nothing short of outright ownership would properly secure the future
and clear the way for their plans for Silverstone. Negotiations
by the club to buy the circuit go back to 1960 and were to continue for a decade before they were completed. The club's records
of the 1950s point to many difficulties but the greatest problem,
other than one of finance, was the Silverstone farm.

The origins of the situation go back to before the war and
in the early post-war years of food shortage and widespread
rationing, the proper use of agricultural land was very much
in the national interest. Silverstone had originally been part of
a farm complex and the Ministry of Aviation had acquired areas
of adjoining land in order to create an airfield. Before racing
there was envisaged, a tenancy agreement for Silverstone had
been acquired by a Mr Graham, a farmer. Initially he grew no
crops, only grass which he harvested and turned into winter
fodder for cattle. Subsequently he added grain crops and even
a battery of hens. He had no right to the runways, other than
rights of way, and a special deal was negotiated in the days of
the RAC tenancy which left the runways and the perimeter road
available for racing, plus the use of certain areas for car parking.

Motor racing and farming are a doubtful combination, but at
Silverstone, where the latter sat almost in the former's lap, the
qualities of co-existence were stretched to the limit. It was a
unique situation which brought its rows, threats, and regular
declarations of intent, and within such a harassing situation an
uneasy truce was the best that could be hoped for.

For both parties it was an almost intolerable situation and the
confrontations were many: but the farmer was a sitting tenant

and could not be dispossessed. He exercised his rights and Jimmy Brown, as the man-on-the-spot, was left to face his wrath. 'Jim's brief was to turn the other cheek, which he did magnificently and with great self-control,' remembers Des Scannell.

Silverstone lived with the situation until 1958–59 when the farmer said he was prepared to sell. Said Des Scannell: 'There was no other way except to buy him out. The asking price seemed a staggering sum in those days and the BRDC simply did not have that kind of money, but the deal went through and the farm was thereafter run profitably in harmony with the racing circuit's prime interest.' Purchase of the farm company had implications more far-reaching than the mere removal of an incompatible neighbour. The Club now had improved security, as a sitting agricultural tenant of the Ministry. But perhaps even more significant was the method adopted for running the farm. Amongst the Club's general committee was a business executive named Peter Clark who lobbied and harassed and cajoled his colleagues into acceptance of the belief that they could not hope to run a successful business by Committee: leave it, he begged, as an ordinary limited company which just happens to be owned by the Club.

This advice was heeded, and has been the pattern upon which the BRDC/Silverstone Group of Companies with five commercial subsidiaries has subsequently been built up.

A Silverstone Trust, considered more than once in earlier years, was established in 1968 through the drive and initiative of Sir Leonard Crossland, then chairman of Ford, in order to provide the BRDC with the money they would need for ultimate acquisition of the freeholds.

Later that same year came Silverstone's most virulent threat to continued existence as a racing circuit: it was listed for consideration as a possible site for London's third airport. How near it came to being lost as a motor racing circuit is debatable, though Silverstone's legal advisers and the management are well aware that the site was nominated by the Stansted Resistance movement as an alternative to their own threatened area. The BRDC and other local landowners formed an association to protest against the proposition, and for seven long, worrying months the possibility made life at Silverstone dismal. Improvements were delayed but finally a reprieve was announced and Silverstone had been saved yet again. Defence considerations worked in its favour as several military airfields would have been hampered by the establishment of a major civil airport there.

In October 1969, shortly after the announcement that the third airport threat was over, the Club made a purchase of 42 acres of freehold land. In 1970, with help from the Silverstone Trust, the Club purchased a further 398 acres of land freehold from the Ministry of Defence. The announcement was made at the club's annual dinner by its president, the Hon Gerald Lascelles. He said: 'I am proud to announce, now that these long and protracted negotiations have been successfully completed, that we shall be able to develop Silverstone along lines befitting Britain's premier circuit.' And an appropriate comment came from the RAC: 'The RAC is delighted that Silverstone circuit is now certain to continue to be available as a motor racing venue. As the circuit where we revived the British Grand Prix in the immediate post-war years, it holds a special place in the affections of motor sport enthusiasts.' Finally in November 1971 a final purchase of 240 acres completed the 700 acre estate.

10

Changes on the Ground

When racing at Silverstone at last received the go-ahead in 1948 there was a massive job to be done and very little time to do it in. The layout of the circuit claimed little priority. After all, the road and runways were already established and the general thought was to use as much of them as possible. Consequently all the perimeter road (except for the two short stretches) and most of the runways, were utilised for that first Grand Prix.

Corners and straights needed identification. Seaman Corner and Segrave Straight were fitting tributes to great British drivers by then departed, while other features were named to link with local landmarks. Adopted in haste, Becketts, Woodcote, Stowe and others were to endure as instant labels to Silverstone at race tracks and in motor racing conversations all over Europe.

No one pretended that Silverstone was perfect. As *Autocar* observed: 'Its very bareness makes it difficult to pick a cut-off point and you almost need a pilot car to find the right hole to go into on the back straight.' But the will was strong and time was to witness vast improvement.

A revised circuit and layout was used for the second Grand Prix in 1949, the initial circuit having exposed its shortcomings when first used. The surface on the runways was not good for racing and use of the runways took cars into the infield and away from the crowds, so for 1949 the runways were not used, the new circuit following the perimeter road. This made it faster and more like the road circuits of Europe. A hazard in the form of a chicane was constructed at Club Corner at the entry to the runway there to pull speeds down, add interest and test the skill of the drivers, but this was not popular and was removed for 1950, never to reappear. *Motor* expressed what many thought: 'What Silverstone lacks is a good straight and, more important,

111

a real slow corner and I do not mean a weird chicane or an artificial S bend. On the other hand, Silverstone, like Monte Carlo, is a unique sort of circuit which drivers begin to enjoy after they have raced there several times.'

The circuit for 1949 measured three miles. Another change was an adjustment to the start line: it was re-positioned just forward of *The Motor* bridge and not behind it as in 1948, and consequent re-siting of the stands and pits, both of which had been considerably enlarged. New stands were built to overlook Becketts, Stowe and the chicane at Club.

By 1950 and the Grand Prix d'Europe, Silverstone ranked as one of the fastest circuits in Europe, in spite of its longest straight being only about 850 yards. The chicane of course had gone and all corners eased as much as possible in radius so that drivers had no reason to drop down to bottom gear on any section of the course. The aim was to recreate as nearly as possible the character of a true road circuit.

Other than the acknowleged straights, the fastest section of the course was Maggotts, beyond which drivers had to brake for Becketts, then surge through the curve of Chapel to thunder down Hangar Straight, the fastest section of the circuit taken at around 120 mph even in 1950. At such a speed Stowe Corner comes up quickly; then follows Club Corner, fairly straightforward. The left-handed Abbey Curve is more sinister than it looks and more than one driver has been astonished to find himself ploughing through the crops there. Then followed the sprint past the pits, about 700 yards, before setting the car up for the four-wheel drift round Woodcote and then on to Copse and, beyond, the straight back to Maggotts.

The International Trophy race was run in 1949 without the chicane, making the course just 2 miles 1,710 yards, and both Ascari in the Ferrari and Bira (Maserati) lapped at more than 93 mph.

Of the eight corners Stowe was originally regarded as the most difficult, positioned at the end of the slight downhill section of the very fast Hangar Straight, and Silverstone's lack of natural features imposed considerable demands on the judgment of drivers here and at many other critical sections. Later, steps were taken to outline the course more clearly and permanently, but at the time only straw bales were used which could easily be moved out of place, and it was difficult to position them accurately anyway. So the course was rather vaguely defined. Drivers did not like straw bales which, along with old oil drums, were used to mark out the inside arch of the curves across the end of the runways, and one vividly held recollection is of Fangio in the 2½ litre Mercedes having a particularly hazardous time in the Grand Prix. He just was not able to aim the Mercedes, with its enveloping body which obscured the front wheels, and kept knocking the oil drums, lap after lap. Later, low walls of concrete blocks were used which were easy to see and, being solid, were held in healthier respect by drivers. Later still, these walls were removed again, in the cause of safety, and today 'sighting for line' on the corners is by means of white plastic flippers set into broad white lines.

Woodcote in those early days was the first corner after the startline, which was positioned at the top of the rise after Abbey Curve, but when the BRDC took over the RAC's lease in 1952, dramatic changes began to take place, in close collaboration with the RAC's motor sport division which continued – and to this day still continues – to carry responsibility for all aspects of safety at British racing circuits.

The idea of moving the pits and the start-finish line to a position around Woodcote corner was part of a proposed new layout drawn up by Kenneth Evans, which also included the erection of earth banks on the corners. Kenneth was the long-standing post-war honorary Surveyor to the Club and a prominent racing driver, before the war, on the international scene. Materials were still scarce, but the advantages from the move were many and were to benefit the club over many years. The whole idea was considered in conjunction with the proposed creation of a shorter 'club circuit' to a new layout from Woodcote to Copse, to Maggotts, to Becketts, and back along a runway to Woodcote, and was based on sound commercial judgment.

For a start it was important to make the co-existence with the farm tenant as harmonious as possible. The new arrangement would keep the disruption of farming activities to a minimum and would make the best possible use of the limited amount of land available from the farm tenant. There was some existing hard standing in the new area, which was useful, and by re-siting the pits and grandstands between Woodcote and Copse the BRDC was immediately able to make use of the club circuit on a greater number of days during the year. They would also be able to make the pits and ancilliary facilities available to both the club and Grand Prix circuits, while also offering some of them for rent to oil and fuel companies on an annual basis.

There was some criticism that the new start/finish line increased the dangers in the pit area, but Desmond Scannell and others thought the original location more dangerous. However, safety reasons were certainly behind the proposal of Stirling Moss for the construction of a slip road to the pits to start from the beginning of Woodcote corner. Stirling's idea received support from Mike Hawthorn and others and certainly improved safety at the pit area.

Woodcote Corner itself presented special problems due to being of 'twin apex' configuration and one remembers Mike Hawthorn's spectacular trouble on the grass in front of the grandstands. Thus in due time the active drivers on the BRDC's General Committee held a day-long testing session, as a result of which the corner became faster but safer since it now had only one apex.

As the circuit was now owned by a club for drivers, much notice was taken of the comments and suggestions of the men who raced at Silverstone and, as Desmond Scannell remarked, being a democratic body ideas were always worth a try. One of the most unusual perhaps was a series of experiments undertaken by Reg Parnell and Graham Whitehead, who tried lapping the circuit anti-clockwise, but it was reported that neither driver favoured the idea. It was also about that time that further experiments were held with a chicane at Woodcote, but these too never got further than the experimental stage. 'They were just ideas,' said Desmond Scannell, 'but it was a good thing to try them out.'

Improved spectator protection was soon recognised as vital to Silverstone with its vast crowds. In 1952 work started on the provision of a ditch about three feet deep of which one side would slope gently towards the road while the other would be vertical and surmounted by a two foot bank. Of course there had been accidents and incidents, but mercifully these had been confined to the track and had been extremely few. Established because there was nothing better at the time, Silverstone rapidly evolved to a high standard of circuit safety with its exceptionally wide track, its open corners, its wide grass verges all the way round and, above all, its first class marshalling and organisation.

Everything still had to be done on a shoestring and the banking which was constructed for spectator safety was done with equipment borrowed from its manufacturer. At first, the protective banking was only at the more popular areas where the biggest crowds foregathered. But the 1955 Le Mans crash pointed up such hideous consequences that there was a scramble to complete the earth banks right round the circuit in time for the start of racing the following season. Needless to say the spectators, although better protected, now had difficulty in seeing the cars, and this problem has only been recently overcome by a continuous programme of 'muck-shovelling', which may continue *ad infinitum*.

Silverstone was indeed in poor shape when the BRDC took over in 1952, barren and exposed and with crude facilities. The air control tower from the airfield days was of course there, but apart from this the scrutineers used a tent and the club was largely dependent on caravans for office space. The first permanent buildings were taken over by the timekeepers and race control, but it was all a very slow business. The underlying problem was that, under the terms of the lease, the airfield would in theory have to be handed back eventually to the Defence Ministry 'in status quo', and thus it was impossible to finance in a normal manner the construction of permanent buildings.

For the 1965 British Grand Prix drivers used for the first time in a Grand Prix race the newly erected ramps in front of the pits. These ramps, designed following an accident in which an official was regrettably killed in front of the pits, gave added security and were a worthwhile bonus for spectators who could get a better view from the grandstand of work being carried on in the pits.

Perhaps Silverstone's most notable achievement is that, after twenty-five years, it is still there – unlike many circuits in many parts of the world, which have rapidly achieved more glamorous installations, and have then found themselves in impossible financial straits.

11

More than Just
a Grand Prix Circuit

To motor race enthusiasts Silverstone means large excited crowds, big races with Formula 1 celebrities like Emerson Fittipaldi, Ronnie Peterson and Graham Hill on view, and all the elaborate trappings of a really major occasion.

Silverstone is acknowledged as one of the truly great Grand Prix circuits. It is also much more than that. For years it has promoted motor racing in the widest sense, initiated trends and catered for a variety of tastes in a professional and spectacular way. It boosted 500 cc motor racing at a critical time for the sport as a whole. There were sports car and saloon car and vintage car races. At the big meetings the special interval entertainment was said by one motoring journalist to be alone worth the money it cost to get into Silverstone.

The circuit is also constantly in use for private practice and testing and is in demand as an authentic location for film and television crews seeking a motor racing situation. In spite of its deep traditions, you cannot call it stuffy. Innovation is welcomed – drag racing and the spectacular caravan races in 1973 for instance.

Silverstone's inner strength comes from its close and lasting involvement with club racing. A club circuit was established in the second year of the circuit's existence and was changed in 1952 when the pits and grandstands were moved to their present position. The original start/finish line was up the runway from Stowe and the circuit took in Copse, then back along the perimeter road into Becketts, Chapel and down Hanger Straight back to Stowe.

The new club circuit of 1952 adopted the Grand Prix start/

finish line and took in the straight to Copse, along through Maggotts and Becketts, then a sharp right hander on to the runway straight to Woodcote and right again to the start/finish.

From the beginning the circuit's deliberate policy was to foster the spirit of clubmen's racing, thereby giving young and promising drivers every opportunity to learn their trade and develop their skills in the atmosphere and environment of the big time. Many top drivers served their apprenticeship at Silverstone.

The role is maintained today and in this way Silverstone is unusual, but not surprising, for the BRDC which owns it is itself a motoring club and organiser of roughly a dozen meetings every year. The intention has always been to make the best possible facilities available, and the circuit is committed to the improvement of motor racing, not to the payment of dividends. In this respect Silverstone is probably unique.

Clubs responded magnificently to the outstretched hand offered by Silverstone and before long were organising races there practically every week-end throughout the year. It became the home of what were then the two most important club races of the season – the Six-Hour Relay Race and the Clubman's Championship. The latter, giving the most successful clubmen the opportunity of driving on the Grand Prix circuit, soon established itself as a showcase for new talent and was an obvious pick-up point for a possible sponsorship the following year.

Through the facilities offered to clubmen, Silverstone's contribution to the ascendancy of Britain in Grand Prix racing is immeasurable. Research, experiment, inspiration – all played a part, but needed to be matched by skill and daring behind the wheel and this was Silverstone's crusade. As a motor racing journalist once reported: 'Great drivers are bred and require a breeding ground. Here Silverstone stands foremost among British racing circuits for throughout the post-war years it provided the opportunity, week-end after week-end, for British drivers to gain the training that is lacking in other countries.'

So exceptional was Silverstone's role in this critical period of motor racing for Britain that the revered giants of Italy and Germany felt disposed to take careful note of what was going on. In both countries steps were urgently taken in 1956 to introduce a junior formula in which to nurture drivers of the future, and one Italian newspaper acknowledged the UK's importance in this way: 'The young British dare-devils are hacking at the pedestals of our motor racing idols. They are the product of the clubs where policies and speeches are unknown, where the teaching is sound, where they carry out long post-mortems after an event and, above all, prepare for the Grand Prix victory of tomorrow. These are the kind of clubs which Italy with its long tradition of great drivers needs today.'

One of the earliest club events held at Silverstone was in July 1949 when the Bugatti Owners Club organised its first 'closed invitation' sports car race meeting on the shorter circuit. By 1952 some fifteen club meetings were held there. By 1968 the figure had risen to 43. Among clubs lucky to find time at Silverstone were the owners clubs of Aston Martin, Austin Healey, Bentley, Jaguar and MG. There were regional motor clubs from Coventry and other parts of Warwickshire, Nottingham, Peterborough and Hertfordshire, and also at Silverstone that year were the Vintage Sports Car Club, the Sporting Owner Drivers' Club, the British Automobile Racing Club, the 750 Motor Club, and others.

Clubmen's races, far from dull and dusty affairs, have a vigour and hairiness all their own and are fought within a tremendous spirit of enthusiasm. Full programmes are arranged like that of the Aston Martin Owners Club at their annual St John Horsfall event on July 7, 1973. Racing began at 2 pm with historic sports and racing car events. Then followed an interesting ten-member event when Aston Martin owners showed their skills in competition with members of the Jaguar Drivers' Club. The programme also included sports car races complying with the HSCC formula, Vintage and Venerable (PVT) Aston Martin and historic racing and sports cars, a special race for post-war Aston Martins with a sealed handicap and a race for invited historic racing cars built before 1940.

The club circuit is by no means the poor relation of the Grand Prix circuit, as was amply demonstrated in the late summer of 1959 during the 63 lap Commander Yorke Trophy Race for Formula 3 cars, which was held on the club circuit. It was one of the most exciting in this famous series. The lead changed many times before Tom Bridger eventually won narrowly from Don Parker. It was virtually the swan song of 500 cc racing and a magnificent note on which to end.

In 1962 26 new lap records in various classes were estab-

lished on the club circuit, ranging from a 57.42 mph lap by
Dave Simmonds on a Tohatsu motor cycle of only 50 cc to Mike
Beckwith's 87.44 mph lap – a circuit record – in a 1100 cc Lotus.
Beckwith set his figures on June 16 at the Nottingham Sports
Car Club's race meeting, a day on which five club circuit records
were to fall. Among them was Beckwith's same-day circuit record
which Brian Hart, in a Formula 2 (1500 cc) Lotus, shattered by
lapping in 1 min 4.6 secs, a speed of 89.61 mph. A couple of
weeks later, Richard Attwood, soon to become a Grand Prix
driver, came close to that time in a Formula Junior Cooper when
he lapped at 1 min 5.4 secs.

The first driver to lap the club circuit at over 90 mph was
Chris Summers in a massive Cooper-Chevrolet, and that was in
1962 also. On September 1 Summers lapped in 1 min
2.6 secs, exactly two seconds faster than Hart and averaging
92.47 mph, a speed which looked as if it might stand for some
time.

The Clubmen's Championship of 1963 was held on the Grand
Prix circuit as usual in October, but before that late-season wind
up, Chris Summers made another mark on club circuit history.
In September, in the Cooper-Chevrolet once again, he lapped in
1 min 0.6 secs, a speed of over 95 mph. It was obviously only a
matter of time before the club circuit would join the ranks of
100 mph courses.

It was Chris Summers yet again in 1965, and once more in
the Cooper-Chevrolet: he reduced the club circuit record to
below the minute, lapping in 59.4 secs to cover the distance at
97.29 mph. Not long before, it seemed, seventy seconds had
been considered a good time for the club circuit, yet at this
time the record for 1172 cc Ford-engined specials was 1 min
11.2 secs – over 81 mph.

Three years later, in 1968, the club circuit reached that 100
mph status when Max Mosley, later to become the M in March,
got his Repco-Brabham Ford, of 1594 cc, round the short circuit in exactly 57 secs, a speed of 101.45 mph. The time was
duplicated by Jim Moore in a 4.7 litre Kincraft, which seemed
to settle the affair.

Always at Silverstone, the motor racing enthusiast can sense
the close unity which exists between the organisers and officials
and the paying customers. They share the same ideals and a

deeply committed love of racing. The Silverstone Club, formed in 1966 to unite the circuit's loyal band of supporters, is an outward expression of this close relationship and has grown in numbers, influence and scope in the intervening years. The club gave its members the opportunity to identify more closely with Silverstone and in return offered special facilities. These now include a discount off grandstand prices at all meetings on the Grand Prix circuit and the chance for club members to drive their road cars on the club circuit. For their annual membership, members also have the exclusive use of the clubhouse overlooking Woodcote Corner at all meetings, plus driving tests, film shows and other social activities during the year.

Any profits earned by the club as a result of serving its members are applied to improving the circuit's amenities. Two fine examples of this co-operation in action have been the presentation of Ambulances to the circuit, and the construction of premises for the British Motor Racing Marshals Club.

The circuit's close ties with all branches of motor sport were started as early as 1949 when the RAC completed arrangements with various governmental ministries and departments for the use of part of the Grand Prix circuit as a test track for the press and manufacturers, and also by motor clubs for speed trials and races.

Another fixture has been the annual test day of the Guild of Motoring Writers. This began at Goodwood, principally as a chance for foreign journalists at the Motor Show to try the new models. It has grown in scope. Rodney Walkerley says a remarkable feature has been the rarity of accidents when enthusiastic motoring writers drive very fast cars round the circuit. Another feature of this occasion, according to Rodney, is the number of writers who refuse to recognise the number of laps allowed on any one car and go on and on, thus depriving other journalists of their chance to drive. 'Odd isn't it,' he says, 'but maybe the excitement grips them and the lust for speed dims their minds.'

The Guild of Motoring Writers discontinued their series of Motor Show test days in 1973, when they went to Beaulieu. It was felt that a high speed test alone did not give the journalists an adequate impression of the family saloons which represent the volume market of our motor industry. The Guild was also conscious that the French or Portugese motoring correspondents from their equivalent of the Chipping Snodgrass Echo did not automatically have the ability to match the lap times put up by John Bolster or Paul Frere. It was well known that certain manufacturers were becoming reluctant to expose their latest models to the unkind treatment to which they were so frequently subjected. The Guild's headquarters, donated by Ford, is situated in the Stewards Enclosure at Silverstone.

Silverstone's tradition brings everybody who is anybody to the circuit and during practice and race days the paddock area becomes the Oxford Circus of motor sport. Similarly, if a car needs testing, if a driver has to be assessed, if a film needs shooting, Silverstone is generally the natural choice. Thousands of publicity pictures have been taken there. Film and television stars have made special journeys to the circuit. When Steve McQueen, racing driver and motor bike fanatic as well as international film star, considered buying a Paul Dunstall Domiracer, he had it tested for him ... at Silverstone. When motor cycle racing star Bill Ivy, sensational on Yamahas during the 1960s, got his first opportunity to ride the famous Japanese factory's machines, it was at works rider Phil Read's invitation ... at Silverstone. In 1973 the Tricentrol Racing Team of Luton announced a startling 200 mph Ford Capri fitted with a 6.4 litre V8 engine producing 530 bhp: it was unveiled to motoring correspondents at Silverstone and had its first race there. When, in the same year, Graham Hill built his own Grand Prix car at enormous expense, he worked desperately hard to have it ready for the GKN meeting at Silverstone, but failed. He was bitterly disappointed, but when the car was ready for its test, it was to Silverstone that he took it.

Numerous documentaries, as well as the more glamorous feature films, have been shot at Silverstone and, again in 1973, when ITV screened *The Team* by John Elliott, the motor racing viewer could see snatches of authentic Silverstone – the race position boards, the bar and clubhouse, the hospitality vans and the nearby airfield.

The interval entertainment at a major meeting has developed into a presentation all its own. It could be claimed that some of the early efforts came close to the bizaree – the time a French cyclist was motorcycle-paced behind a big shield by Geoff Duke and, using an enormous gear higher than one to one, gradually lapped faster and faster and flashed past the stands at approaching 80 mph!

Less of a novelty was the demonstration by Piero Taruffi of the twin-boom Italcorsa, an extraordinary machine which just two months before had captured two international class records, and Goldie Gardner's demonstration of his record-breaking car – their joint appearance was the subject of a most amusing cartoon by Giles, published in the *Express*.

Rover's Turbine Car, Ford of America's 200 mph Ford GT intended to be the Le Mans challenger, and the Allard 'Dragster Dragon' were also shown at Silverstone and at the International Trophy meeting of 1962 the Mercedes Benz 1939 Formula 1 challenger was brought out to perform a series of demonstration laps. Successful cars in sports car and saloon car events and the major international rallies have also been demonstrated.

Often the demonstrations are linked to significant dates or topical occasions. April 1968 marked the 25th anniversary of the opening of Silverstone as a wartime airfield. When karting first became popular, Silverstone arranged an exciting demonstration – they were announced as the 'swarming bumble bees'.

One of the funniest demonstrations involved the BMC mini and that great wit Graham Hill. It was when the mini was still an exciting new idea. The plan was for all the leading Grand Prix drivers to climb inside a mini apiece and do a demonstration lap as a publicity stunt. Straightforward enough. But the organisation had reckoned without the impishness of racing drivers with Hill in their midst. They all agreed to be in reverse gear at the start and when the flag dropped they would shoot off backwards. As Graham said: 'It was terribly funny. Of course, everyone had to be sure that everyone else was going to play the game.'

When eventually the drivers began what was intended to be a demonstration lap in forward gear, it rapidly developed into an out and out race. The minis were going into corners three abreast and down the straights four or five in line touching one another. There were lots of bumps and bashes, but it was very exciting and a wild success.

With its mainline entertainment Silverstone broke new ground in 1973 with the first drag race meeting to be held at the circuit on the main straight of the club circuit. The event was organised by the National Drag Racing Club as one of six NDRC championship rounds and special stands were erected to accommodate spectators. A quarter mile section of the club circuit was used, starting from Woodcote corner and running in the reverse direction to the racing circuit.

Running this event close for excitement were the Caravan Races in April. This was another 'first' for Silverstone, for such races had never before been run in Britain. They were indeed spectacular, with cars pulling caravans raced round the club circuit at speeds of up to 95 mph in third gear. Said one report: 'Crowds cheered and clapped their new heroes' grand prix style through two races and twenty laps of super spectacle.' The new heroes were undoubtedly Brian Charig in a Mustang GT and Colin Grewer in a ten-year-old hot Volvo. Their dogfight continued throughout the race and one particular report captured the special excitement of this new-style racing: 'Grewer's incredible six-wheel drift as he hurtled through the bends held the growling Mustang at bay. But it was revenge with champagne for Charig whose power on the straights took him to the trophy by just two yeards.' Good stuff indeed.

Nowadays Silverstone is almost constantly active, seven days a week and the activity is so varied that never is one week exactly the same as the next.

Silverstone's aim in meeting the challenge of the seventies is to broaden its interests while fully maintaining its status as the premier circuit, in the country. It remains a great Grand Prix circuit, but by careful development along equally carefully prepared lines, Silverstone has brought the family to the circuit to see the big races. The British Grand Prix meeting of July 1973 was billed as a family day out and incorporated entertainment for the whole family. A 5,000 square foot marquee housed displays and demonstrations of fashion, cosmetics, jewellery, hosiery, Finnish saunas and an Indian boutique. There was a funfair featuring dodgems, roundabouts, speedways sideshows and a wall-of-death. Throughout the three days of the meeting there were continuous programmes of films featuring previous Grands

Prix, and displays more allied to the racing attracted over forty exhibitors and showed motorised homes, caravans, motor accessories, leisure clothing and equipment, books and magazines. For spectators wishing to camp at the circuit a special site was set up.

More than just a Grand Prix circuit? You could say that.

12

The Fastest Circuit

Motor racing means speed and there is more of that at Silverstone than anywhere else in Britain. It was considered a remarkable feat when Villoresi secured the very first fastest lap at 76.82 mph; and so it was, achieved over the 2.9 miles circuit which included the runways. In 1949 and on the circuit without the runways but incorporating the chicane, Bira added 4 mph to the record: and at Royal Silverstone of 1950, on the circuit without the chicane, Farnia reached a record lap of 94.02 mph.

In three short years of the British Grand Prix more than 17 mph had been added to the circuit lap record. Even so, Farina moved the record up dramatically the very next year, reaching 99.99 mph. By now the best cars were averaging about 90 mph. It was virtually flat out all the way round and engines were put to considerable strain. Many simply were not up to it and there were plenty of blow-ups. Tyres took a hammering. The strains were exceptional, but the thoroughbreds stood the distance and speeds continued to rise. By 1958, marking ten years of racing at Silverstone, Mike Hawthorn lapped his Ferrari at over 104 mph and Peter Collins *averaged* more than 102 mph and 101 mph to win the Grand Prix and the International Trophy Meetings. Ten years later Jackie Stewart was a new hero with a record practice lap of 130.73 mph, a new race lap record of 129.60 mph and an average race speed of 127.25 mph.

By 1973 the best speeds at Silverstone were approaching 140 mph and *Competition Car* wondered how long it would be before some cautionary brake would have to be applied in the form of a chicane or two to 'clip the wings of our Grand Prix heroes'. A chicane again after twenty-five years? What sacrilege in the name of progress.

After Farina had driven so close to it in 1951, it took him

two more years to become the first to achieve that magical 100 mph lap. He made it at 100.6 mph in the Thinwall Special. In 1956 Stirling Moss won the International Trophy race at an average speed in excess of Farina's fastest of three years before, and did fastest lap in the same race in a Vanwall at 105 mph. It was a good year for Stirling for he raced to the fastest lap in the British Grand Prix reaching 102.1 mph in a Maserati.

By now Silverstone was famous for its fast driving. Speed was the sensation at the two major anniversary meetings of 1958 when the circuit celebrated its tenth birthday. In the Trophy race Peter Collins (1st), Roy Salvadori (2nd) and Masten Gregory (3rd) all averaged more than 101 mph and in the British Grand Prix Peter Collins won at more than 102 mph with a works Ferrari, the first time that a 100 mph average had been reached in the British classic. Mike Hawthorn was second with an average of 101.73 mph and Roy Salvadori was third with an average of 101.39 mph. Hawthorn was fastest for one lap when he flashed the Ferrari round at 104.54 mph.

These were electrifying speeds for 1958, to be seen only at Silverstone. Technical development in engines, tyres and suspensions coupled with increased knowledge of aerodynamics and lightening processes lifted race speeds not only in the major and fastest events, but right through the in-depth Silverstone programme. In 1958, for instance, Graham Hill won the Sports Car race (up to 1500 cc) at an average of 93.07 mph, while Masten Gregory in the Lister-Jaguar reached an average of 99.54 mph in the over 1500 cc category. In the twenty-laps Touring Car Race, winner Mike Hawthorn averaged 84.22 mph and the 500 cc race was won by Jim Russell at a race average of 89.70 mph – more than 12 mph faster than Villoresi's Grand Prix fastest lap of ten years earlier.

For the following year, 1959, the programme for the International Trophy race saw a significant change. For the first time the 500 cc Formula 3 cars, which had romped round Silverstone at ever-increasing speeds and which were almost certainly the first cars ever to race there (unofficially, in 1947) were not provided with a race. Formula 3, dominated by one make of chassis and one engine, had developed way beyond its original brief to provide low-cost motor-racing: the public were becoming bored by it and it was disappearing fast. It left the scene quietly and without fuss – sad, in view of the contribution these astonishing little cars had made to the cause of motor racing.

So, in May 1959 there was no race for them. They gave way to a 12-lap event for Grand Touring cars and where Coopers and double-knocker Nortons used to blip and thunder, Turners, Austin-Healeys, MG's, Lotuses, Aston Martins and Morgans now rumbled and screamed throatily and threateningly. Stirling Moss, making the competition debut of the DB4 Aston Martin, took an immediate lead and kept in front all way to win from Salvadori's Jaguar and Colin Chapman's Lotus Elite. Moss's fastest lap, in 1 min. 55.8 secs, was the first of many records to be broken or equalled that day: four more went in the Touring Car race, Ivor Bueb (who won) starting proceedings with a lap in 1 min 59.2 seconds. Bob Gerard broke another by getting his A35 saloon round in 2 mins 16.0 secs. Gunnar Bengtsson, in a Volvo, set new figures for the 1600 cc category with a lap in 2 mins 13.8 secs and in the up to 2600 cc class Peter Blond's 2 mins 6.0 secs lap was another.

Formula Junior, a single-seater category which had had its origins in Italian club racing, was given international status for 1959. The Fiat power units adopted in Italy were not universally admired or even available elsewhere in Europe, but since the Formula merely laid down that the main components should be taken 'from normal production cars' there was no lack of a substitute.

Formula Junior made its Silverstone debut at the International Trophy meeting in May, 1960, with a dozen makes (in which Cooper, Lotus and Lola were dominant, supported by Envoy, Gemini, Elva and others) using engines which in the main came from Austin A35 and Ford Anglia Saloons. A good many of the drivers were familiar from 500 cc racing, too, but the big names were not there – barred by a regulation specifically designed to keep the Junior formula 'junior', as a training ground for new talent. At Silverstone Trevor Taylor did the fastest practice lap in 1 min 47.2 secs, a speed of just over 98.2 mph and a bit more than a second quicker than a young Scot by the name of Jim Clark. Another man named John Surtees got a Cooper round in 1 min 51 secs, and when the 27 starters left the grid Taylor and Clark's Lotuses led from Surtees and Henry Taylor. Retirements were many in this first race – fourteen cars finished, and at the end Clark won from Surtees, with another famous motor cyclist, Geoff Duke, seventh.

But it was not really the Junior race which caught the attention of the crowd. In private practice before the event Jack Brabham, it had been reported, had lowered the lap record unofficially by five seconds, lapping at 111 mph in a new Cooper which he was due to drive in the race itself. Practice proved nothing. Cold, wet weather kept speeds down and Moss was fastest in 1 min 50.4 secs. He shared the front row of the grid with the BRMs of Bonnier and Dan Gurney and Phil Hill's Ferrari. Way back on the end of the third row of the grid was a Scot by the name of Innes Ireland, in a rear-engined Lotus, but there was nothing to suggest that he was going to win the fastest race ever run at Silverstone and crack the lap record wide open in doing so.

After only three laps Moss, leading from Ireland and Brabham, was lapping at over 107 mph – well inside the record, and then did 1 min 36.8 secs (108.86 mph) to which Brabham replied by lapping in 1 min 36 secs exactly: over 109 mph. Ireland, in second place, began to put on the pressure: Moss, in turn, responded, and down came the record once more. Stirling went round in 1 min 35.0 secs, a speed of over 110 mph and five seconds better than the existing record – a record which was beginning to seem slow. After ten laps the race *average* speed was a couple of miles an hour faster than Behra's single lap!

Ireland, however, was intent on making history, and started to gain on Moss, lapping at an incredible 1 min 34.2 secs – a speed of 111.86 mph. When Moss's front suspension collapsed on the Cooper, there was no one in reach of Ireland's Lotus. With only the first three cars on the same lap Ireland won, despite Brabham's all-out efforts, by a couple of seconds and at an average speed of 108.82 mph. All three of the first men home – third was Graham Hill's BRM – averaged a higher speed for the whole 150 miles than the old lap record, and during the race no fewer than eleven drivers beat the previous figures.

The next major event was the British Grand Prix, which resulted in a win for Brabham after a tremendous race with Graham Hill's BRM which ended when Hill spun at Copse. The race speed was 108.69 mph, the fastest lap – by Hill – 111.62 mph, just two-tenths above Ireland's record. At other times in

the day, the 1100 cc lap record for sports cars came down to
1 min 46.0 secs – 99.41 mph and the Formula Junior lap record
was broken four times to come down to 1 min 45.8 secs –
99.60 mph.

Conditions were appalling, too, for the International Trophy
meeting in May, 1961, when the main event was for Inter-
Continental formula cars with engines of up to three litres'
capacity. A notable newcomer was a new, rear-engined Vanwall
driven by John Surtees, which proved to be very fast in practice.
Pole position on the grid was occupied by Bruce McLaren's
Cooper, which had equalled the lap record in 1 min 34.2 secs.
But when the cars came to the start it was pouring with rain,
and for once motor-racing's rapidly complicated technology was
caught napping. The rain tyres then newly developed by Dun-
lop were available for Formula 1 cars but not for Inter-
Continental machines, and thus normal tyres had to be fitted. In
such conditions cars spun off easily. An early lead by reigning
World Champion Jack Brabham was eventually taken over by
Stirling Moss and the race then became a demonstration by
Stirling of how to go very quickly in the wet. Brabham was content to stay in a secure second place.

May 12th, 1962, the date of the fourteenth International
Trophy meeting, was something of an anniversary for Silverstone
– the meeting was the twenty-first big international meeting run
there. The event was for Formula 1 cars – the 1500 cc Formula
1 which created so much argument and controversy when it was
introduced for the previous season. Five BRMs – three from the
'works' for Graham Hill, Richie Ginther and Tony Marsh, plus
a brace of private entries – a works Cooper and three privateers,
a Ferrari, a Porsche, two Lolas, two Emerysons and a whole
gaggle of Lotuses lined up, one of the latter being entered by
Brabham Racing Organisation and driven by Jack Brabham,
World Champion Cooper driver. No one was quite sure how the
little Grand Prix cars would fare but they were expected to be at
least as quick as the old Formula 2 machines of the same engine
capacity. The lap record for those cars stood for a couple of
years or so at 1 min 43.4 secs, a speed of 101.91 mph. As it
turned out, Jim Clark soon rectified any misunderstandings there
might be in that direction : he went round seven seconds faster
than the old Formula 2 car and his record lap of 1 min 36.4 secs

E

was a speed of 109.31 mph. In the race itself, one of the closest the circuit had ever seen, he gained second place behind Graham Hill's BRM. Both cars were credited with an identical average speed for the race at 99.73 mph.

Clark's was not the only record lap of the day. In the Grand Touring car race, fought out between Turners, Sebring Sprites, Marcos, Lotus, Porsches, Morgans, and, in the over 2-litre class, three Ferraris, four Aston Martins and five Jaguars, five new lap records were established, including the setting up of the first lap at 100 mph–plus, by a closed car. This went to Mike Parkes, whose Ferrari went round in 1 min 43.2 seconds – 102.10 mph. Not far behind was Graham Hill, whose Jaguar broke the 3500–5000 cc record at 1 min 45.8 secs, 99.60 mph. And Trevor Taylor (Lotus Elite), Dick Stoope (Porsche) and Chris Lawrence (Morgan) also broke class records, Lawrence knocking some four seconds off his own record to put a 2-litre G.T. car into the over 90 mph lap bracket for the first time.

The International Trophy race in 1963 was won by Jim Clark who covered the 52 laps at 108.12 mph. Second was Bruce McLaren's Cooper, with another Lotus driven by Trevor Taylor, in third place. And the Grand Touring car lap record was broken again : Parkes, again in a Ferrari, lowered his own time to 1 min 42.8 secs (102.50 mph), but another Grand Tourer joined the three-figure lap speed and went even faster. Roy Salvadori's Jaguar went round in 1 min 42.4 seconds to average 102.90 mph. It was one of three records broken by Salvadori that day : in a 2½-litre Cooper sports car he did 1 min 37.6 (107.96 mph) and in the touring car race, he got his Jaguar 3.8 round in 1 min 54.2 Secs, 92.97 mph.

In July, 1963 the British Grand Prix at Silverstone witnessed Jim Clark in practice, wasting very little time, going round in 1 min 34.4 secs, just two-tenths of a second outside the outright lap record – on the first day. No one was able to improve on him in the race itself, as might have been expected. He took the lead after three laps and gave everyone a driving lesson thereafter. It was one of a series of brilliant results which gave him the 1963 World Championship.

The Grand Prix circuit season for 1964 opened, as usual, with the International Trophy meeting in May. Two Brabhams, a BRM and a Lotus, driven by Jack Brabham himself, Dan Gurney,

Graham Hill and Jim Clark, shared the front row of the grid, and for once it wasn't Jim Clark's day. Brabham ran out winner by a short head from Hill, with Peter Arundell's Lotus third.

Brabham broke the Formula 1 record and, in so doing, set new figures for the outright circuit record. He lapped in 1 min 33.6 secs to put the average lap speed over 112 mph for the first time – 112.56, to be precise. More class records went during a sports car meeting held on the full circuit in July that year, but the record for record-breaking was established at the end of the season in the Clubman's Championship event, when no fewer than seven records were established. Two cars, a Lotus and a Brabham driven by Fenning and Mac, set up figures for the new Formula 3 at 1 min 44.2 secs, a speed of 101.12 mph compared with the earlier 500 cc Formula 3 record of 92.43 mph which was established by Stuart Lewis-Evans in 1958. And Chris Summers, this time in a Chevrolet-powered Lotus, lapped in 1 min 36.6 secs, 109.08 mph, in the Formula Libre race, while other drivers set new class figures in the touring and grand touring car events.

For once the International Trophy meeting did not open the Grand Prix circuit for 1965 – the British Automobile Club ran its International 200-miles race there in March – but it remained the first big meeting in Britain at which the Formula 1 cars and drivers turned out. The line-up on the grid included the reigning World Champion John Surtees, Jackie Stewart supporting Graham Hill in the BRM team, Dennis Hulme and Jack Brabham in Brabhams and a new Austrian discovery, Jochen Rindt, backing Bruce McLaren for Coopers. It was a fast race which Jackie Stewart won. He covered the 152 miles in under 82 minutes to cross the line at an average speed of 111.66 mph, finishing three seconds in front of Surtees' Ferrari with Mike Spence, in a Lotus, nearly a minute behind in third place.

Fast it certainly was, but the British Grand Prix, run at Silverstone in July, was even faster. Practice showed the shape of what was to come in this, the last British Grand Prix to be held for the 1½-litre Formula 1 cars. Pole position on the grid went to Jim Clark, whose Lotus had lapped in 1 min 30.8 secs – just over 116 mph. And a dozen other cars had bettered the record of 1 min 33.6 secs set up by Brabham a year ago while Innes Ireland had equalled it – and he was back on the fifth row of the grid! Clark was to win the race, the fastest ever run at

Silverstone, at over 112 mph – only slightly slower than that twelve months old lap record – and finished a little over three seconds in front of Graham Hill, with John Surtees third. Clark in fact was slowed by falling oil pressure after sixty of the eighty laps of the race, and Hill tried hard to catch him – hard enough, in fact, to bring the lap record down to 1 min 32.2 secs – a speed of 114.29 mph, despite having largely ineffective brakes.

Graham Hill's 1 min 32.2 seconds lap was to stand for all time as the 1½-litre Formula 1 lap record, but it lasted less than a year as a circuit record. On May 14th 1966, three events took high speed motoring at Silverstone into a new and sensational era. Chris Amon, driving a McLaren sports car, did a lap in 1 min 30.8 secs (116.05 mph) to take nearly eleven seconds off the 4000–5000 cc sports car record at the International Trophy meeting. Dramatic enough, since apart from this it was also substantially faster than the existing single-seater record. But in the same race Denny Hulme, in a Lola, set a sports car record for over 5000 cc-engined cars in an unbelievable 1 min 28.8 secs, a shattering speed of 118.66 mph.

So the outright lap record was at this point held by a sports car. What could the Formula 1 cars, coming to the grid in new 3-litre form for the first time, do about that? The answer was, apparently, nothing. Oh yes, the racing car record was broken – smashed wide open, in fact, and a racing car joined the under ninety-seconds league when Jack Brabham, in his new F1 car, went round in 1 min 29.8 seconds, at 117.34 mph. But Hulme's time was still quicker.

With the 1966 British Grand Prix at Brands Hatch, Silverstone's lap records were left untouched for the remainder of that year. But some of them did not survive very long in 1967.

The first meeting of 1967 on the Silverstone Grand Prix circuit was the Wills Trophy meeting at the end of March, the main event being run for Formula 2 cars. The Formula 1 brigade took a step further away from their position as the fastest things on wheels in Northamptonshire when Graham Hill, in an F2 Lotus, and Jochen Rindt in an F2 Brabham (the latter winning the race on aggregate of two heats), each lapped in 1 min 29.2 seconds, six-tenths faster than Brabham's Formula 1 record, and an average speed of over 118 mph – figures now beaten only by Hulme's big sports car and the F2 single-seaters. Rindt's race average was over 116 mph.

A month later, at the end of April, the Formula 1 cars came out again for the International Trophy meeting, but records stayed intact. Mike Parkes, in a Ferrari, won the 152-mile main race at 114.6 mph from Brabham and Jo Siffert, in a Cooper-Maserati. Fastest lap was set by Graham Hill in a Lotus-BRM, but his time of 1 min 30.0 secs (117.08 mph) was not quick enough for the record book. It almost seemed that Hulme's time was to be an ultimate record.

But the British Grand Prix on July 15th 1967, soon put that right. In the first practice period the Formula 1 cars began to show their paces. Brabham was fastest, with a lap in 1 min 26.6 secs to take the speed over 120 mph. Ten years before, Hawthorn and Moss held the Formula 1 record jointly at just over 102 mph – now Brabham had lapped, admittedly an unofficial practice speed, at 121.68 mph; and six other drivers equalled Hulme's record in this first session. In the second period, during the afternoon of the same day, Jim Clark was fastest, knocking a tenth of a second off Brabham's time, but that was not all. In the third and final practice period, on the day before the race, Clark improved by over a second to gain pole position on the grid with a time of 1 min 25.3 secs – over 123 mph, and the next four fastest cars were all inside Brabham's 1 min 26.6 secs. When the grid was established, all the cars in the first three rows had bettered Hulme's record. Given a dry circuit for the race, it was clearly going to be a very fast eighty laps.

So it proved. At the end, less than two hours after the start, Jim Clark crossed the line first having averaged 117.64 mph – faster than Brabham's Formula 1 lap record. Graham Hill, whose Lotus had been running nose to tail with Clark's similar car at the head of the field, was delayed by rear suspension trouble and finally put out by engine failure. Second place went to Hulme's Brabham-Repco, a quarter-minute behind. But Hulme had the consolation of a new lap record, established as fastest lap of the race on lap three. He went round in 1 min 27.0 seconds, not quite as quick as practice had promised, but still fast enough to bring the Silverstone circuit record speed up and beyond the 121 mph mark. The outright record was once again with Grand Prix cars.

That was 1967. In 1968 Silverstone was better and faster. At the end of the season there was a new circuit and Formula 1 record, and new figures for the records in twelve other categories. The first and fastest came in April, at the International Trophy meeting, in which the McLarens of Hulme and McLaren, in that order, finished first and second, while the lap record went to Chris Amon's Ferrari. Amon made all previous performances look slow by rocketing round nearly two seconds faster than anyone had ever gone before to record a time of 1 min 25.1 secs – 123.82 mph. He took third place in the race.

It was a fast-moving day, and Hulme's overall average speed for the race, at 122.17 mph, meant that he was lapping steadily and constantly at better than the previous lap record of less than a year ago. Brian Muir won even the saloon car race at over 101 mph; in fact, with one exception, every race on the programme was run at over 100 mph.

In July a meeting on the Grand Prix circuit for Formula 3, sports and touring cars set twelve lap records, although the outright record was safe enough, for the time being. The new figures ranged from Frank Gardener's 1 min 28.6 secs (118.93 mph) in the Ford 3-litre prototype Group 6 sports car, to Bill Morris' lap in an ERA at 1 min 54.8 secs (91.79 mph) which set a new record for pre-war historic racing cars.

The International Trophy race in 1969 was run on a wet track, and the figures stayed as they were, which meant that when the British Grand Prix came to Silverstone on July 19th the outright record had stood for over a year – a long time for a Silverstone record.

Given good weather, everyone was prepared for the record to fall. No one was prepared, however, for the sort of times which were recorded during practice. These times do not, of course, count as records, but they show what can be done under the right conditions. By race day, the official lap record had been bettered so often that nothing short of a miracle could have sustained it, and when the grid formed up only three cars – oddly all of them with four-wheel-drive – had failed to lap at or below the record. Fastest of all was Jochen Rindt, whose staggering time of 1 min 20.8 secs was the first lap at over 130 mph ever recorded on any British circuit, other than the banked Brooklands track. Jackie Stewart, who was to win the race and the World

Championship for Matra and Ken Tyrrell, did 1 min 21.2 secs, while right back in row six of the grid John Miles, a newcomer to Formula 1 and driving the largely untried four-wheel-drive Lotus, had equalled the record with a time of 1 min 25.1 secs.

The race itself was gripping: Rindt and Stewart fought like tom-cats for over sixty laps until the rear aerofoil wing on the former's Lotus necessitated a pit-stop for adjustment. He went back into the race still in second place, for he and Stewart had lapped the entire field at least once after 56 laps. Then he ran short of fuel just before the end of the race, which left Stewart to sail home a full lap ahead of Jacky Ickx, in second place. But the speeds which Stewart and Rindt had reached during their dog-fight were astounding: these were not achieved at carefully selected practice times with little traffic about but in the heat of racing, with cars all round the circuit. The record fell time after time, Stewart finally leaving it at 1 min 21.3 secs – fractionally below 130 mph, while Rindt's best was just one-tenth of a second slower.

Because of Rindt's various troubles with the Lotus, Stewart was able to ease off in the last couple of laps. But that did not stop him from averaging 127.25 mph, once again the fastest race ever run in Britain post-war. It was over 3½ mph faster – after 246 miles – than Chris Amon's previous record for just one lap!

Surely the ultimate had been reached? Not yet. Not quite. Chris Amon in the March fell short in the International Trophy event of 1970 at 128.35 mph, but a commanding Jackie Stewart made 1971 his own special year at Silverstone. In the former event he flashed round at 130.9 mph and did even better in the Woolmark British Grand Prix. He created a new race lap record on lap 45, returning 1 min 19.9 secs – an incredible 131.88 mph. By this time the practice lap record had rocketed to 136.847 mph, reached by Australian Frank Gardner in June 1971 driving a 7.9 litre Lola T260 – Chevrolet Group 7 sports car.

This practice lap record was held by Gardner well into 1972, but Jackie's race lap record was to be short lived. Mike Hailwood, who years earlier had known his way round Silverstone on motor bikes, cracked it open at the International Trophy meeting on April 23, 1972. He rocketed the 2.993 cc Surtees-Cosworth V8 down the straights and round the bends and back again in just 1 min 18.8 secs, to reach, for the first time at Silverstone, an incredible race lap speed of 122.72 mph. In ten years Silverstone had got faster by more than 24 mph and in twenty years was quicker by 45 mph.

For years Silverstone had been Britain's fastest circuit. Now it was reputed as one of the fastest in Europe. Emerson Fittipaldi, the world champion, upheld its distinction in 1973, becoming the fastest driver there ever. The speed ace from Brazil rushed his John Player Team Lotus round in 1 min 16.4 secs, 137.92 mph. taking pole position for the GKN/*Daily Express* Silver Jubilee International Trophy race.

But that of course was in practice and Hailwood still held the official fastest lap record. For how long was anybody's guess.

Simply to say that a new race lap record has been established at Silverstone captures nothing of the drama, tension, skill, concentration and sheer strength of character as well as body, required to create such a record. You appreciate it more when you see it happen from the grandstand, but you would have to be sitting in the car with the driver to experience the realism of Silverstone record breaking . . . if you were not too scared to open your eyes!

12

My Silverstone

The history of Silverstone is crowded with personal reminiscences of great humour, charm, fascination, excitement, sensation and drama. Among those with stories to tell are Jimmy Brown, Rob Walker, Desmond Scannell, Graham Hill, Stirling Moss and Rodney Walkerley.

Many, in the beginning, were concerned with Silverstone's problems in becoming established. Though the problems gradually became less towering and more infrequent, there were still plenty of unforeseen surprises. At one early Grand Prix Jimmy Brown was rushing about crossing off last-minute jobs from his checklist as the crowds poured into the circuit. The car-park chief, an RAC road manager, approached him in a panic to tell him there was a bomb in one of the car parks. It might have been a bomb or it might not, but on a war-time airfield there was always the possibility and Jim could take no chances. A couple of policemen were despatched to the car park where the bomb was found to be a practice dummy. It could have been worse, for in some parts of the airfield there had been bombs and ammunition lying dumped – all very lively, too, after several years of neglect, and there were thousands of people around and more arriving by the minute.

Other problems concerned spectators. At Grand Prix meetings the medical team could expect to deal with several hundred calls on their services, relatively few of which might have any direct connection with the day's racing. When the V16 BRM appeared at the circuit, the tremendous noise made by its exhaust upset many of the spectators, and, as mentioned earlier, the medical crews dealt with over a hundred people who had stuffed wads of paper and cloth into their ears – and could not get them out again. Once an ambulance was called for a man who had broken a limb in the car park, not, it seemed on the face of it, an easy thing to achieve. He had been watching the race in bright sunshine and sunstroke had caused him to fall off the roof of the coach he had chosen as a vantage point. Perhaps surprisingly, records suggest that no babies have yet been born at Silverstone, although there have been some 'near misses' reported: but on one occasion a man in the crowd managed to develop acute appendicitis, calling for some rapid action.

The bumper-to-bumper traffic going into the circuit for international meetings has brought its share of odd occurrences. Two girls were driving along the Towcester road in close traffic, which was controlled by police, of course. With little chance to do anything else, they followed the queue all the way to a Silverstone car park, where they complained bitterly that they had really wanted to go to Banbury! Another car reached the circuit under similar circumstances, and on arrival at the car park two very disappointed football fans jumped out brandishing Cup Final tickets – their original destination had been Wembley!

Early on, when the grandstands were even more temporary than they might have been in less difficult times, strong gales during one of the practice periods weakened the tarpaulin roof of one of the grandstands, and the circuit staff watched helplessly as large pieces of roof simply blew away, piece by piece. This was on the eve of race-day. Somehow the stand was stripped and rebuilt before morning.

Some of the oddest, and at the time among the most worrying, adventures have concerned Royal visits. In 1950, when King George VI visited the circuit with members of the Royal Family, the problems were enormous. Security arrangements had to be worked out and vetted by the Palace, special grandstands and tents were erected, and the Royal Standard had to be brought from London and flown at the appropriate moment. When the time came to hoist the Standard, it was nowhere to be found. Panic was unbridled until it turned up.

Private testing has been carried out on the circuit since the beginning, and today it is in use for either testing or actual competition just about every day of the week unless some major structural alteration forces its temporary closing. It is in private testing that problems have often arisen. In the earliest days there were occasional alarms when local sheep or cattle wandered about on the circuit; fortunately on race days the worst cases of such trespass have been the occasional hare. It was apparently one of these insignificant little animals which put Jean Behra out of a race. Travelling at speed down Hangar Straight his car hit one. The hare, albeit posthumously, had its revenge. One of its bones punctured a tyre and Behra was put out of the running by the resultant pit-stop.

Behra was unlucky when it came to animals at Silverstone. One winter's day the BRM team, with Behra and Harry Schell, arrived at the circuit for a test session with the $2\frac{1}{2}$-litre front-engined BRM. When Behra took it out onto the circuit he was soon back, complaining of horses and dogs all over the place. Investigation revealed that the local hunt were having a check of their own, and an emissary was urgently despatched to ask the Master to get his hounds out of the place.

The BRM, on its first appearance at the circuit, was lucky to escape another, potentially more serious, adventure. This was the occasion already related when, after frantic telephone calls, the machine was flown into Bicester on the morning of race day, police-escorted to Silverstone and then got to the grid with just seconds to go before the start. When the noise and dust of the Grand Prix start had subsided, it became apparent that the BRM had not, in fact, gone with the rest, and with the pack now howling through Becketts the Clerk of the Course demanded that the car, with its attendant gathering of anxious mechanics and others, be moved from the middle of the track. The start at that time was the old one, between Abbey Curve and Woodcote. Close to it was the time-keeper's 'office', an old double-decker bus which, for years afterwards, stood forlorn and neglected in the centre of the airfield. The bus was protected against off-course excursions of cars leaving Abbey by means of a protective barrier, and it was behind this barrier that the BRM and its friends was taken. Barely was it safely there when the leaders, with Johnny Claes among them in his Lago-Talbot, arrived at high speed. Coming out of Abbey, Claes lost it in a monumental fashion, slid off the course and smote the barrier good and hard. And just the other side of it was the BRM – and a crowd of about forty people.

The work of maintaining the circuit and its equipment throughout the year is a continuous process, not unlike the painting of the Forth Bridge. It is complicated in that the racing season now extends from early March until the first week-end in December, so that all the major work has to be crowded into a matter of three months – when generally the weather can be relied on to be at its worst and outside work to be most difficult. A lot of the equipment is dismantled, and taken into dry workshops for repairs, the advertisement hoardings are handled by outside contractors, but gates and fences, grandstands and car parks still have to be attended to by the maintenance team. When major alterations are necessary, as in 1964 when the pit apron was built, and at the end of 1970 when safety arrangements were overhauled, the work schedule is formidable indeed.

Most of the major work is undertaken by local contractors, who have been associated with the circuit over a period of years and have become accustomed to the particular problems. The relationships which have been developed with outside contractors means that rush jobs which are apparently impossible can actually be achieved in little more time than any other miracle might occupy. In the last practice session before the 1969 Grand Prix for instance, Jean-Pierre Beltoise came round Woodcote corner in his Matra and removed a large chunk of concrete from the retaining wall. A few minutes later Jackie Stewart, going very fast indeed, picked up the concrete and crashed heavily into the bank opposite the pits. Clearly, the circuit damage had to be made good, despite the fact that it was 5 p.m. on the day before the race. Contractors came in that night and worked on into darkness until the job was done.

Then there is the farm to be run. Nowadays, and for more than ten years, the farm has been carried on by the BRDC through a subsidiary, and this has eased the problem of dovetailing agriculture with motor-racing. It was not always so, as already recorded, and many testing sessions during the week have been the scene of narrow escapes by all concerned when a farm worker failed to appreciate the proximity of a racing car travelling at 150 mph when backing a tractor and trailer across the track. There have been some abrasive moments between farmers and racers when crops have been damaged by cars spinning off into the wheat, to be accompanied in due time by marshalls, breakdown vehicles and fire-fighting equipment.

Rob Walker, one of the most well-known and respected patrons of motor racing, has close and abiding ties with Silverstone. One of his earliest recollections is of an unpleasant experience after one of the early races and following his return to the Kings Arms at Bicester, where he was staying the night. He was sitting down to dinner when someone said: 'You heard Roy Salvadori was killed today?'

'Who is Roy Salvadori', was the general response.

'A motor trader who has recently taken up racing.' Roy had crashed badly in his Frazer Nash, but the report was incorrect. He had been injured, not killed. He was virtually unknown then, but the incident remained a vivid memory to Rob and never allowed him to forget who Roy Salvadori was, this great driver later turning out in Rob's colours when he was much more famous.

It seems unjust that for all Rob Walker's outstanding contribution to motor racing, he has been consistently unlucky at Silverstone. His single memory of success recalls 1961 and the Intercontinental Formula when Rob still had a 2½ litre Climax running with Stirling Moss at the wheel. It was a filthy day and Stirling made no mistake about it. He lapped the whole field and appropriately Rob has an enlargement picture of the presentation showing Moss receiving the cup with Rob Walker alongside and the late Chief Constable John Gott (how sadly he is missed) in uniform in the background.

Rob Walker did much to pioneer the 2½-litre Copper Climax in the late 1950s. 'Everybody said it was a silly little toy and would never do any good,' he recalls. 'But there was the occasion when Tony Brooks managed to make fastest time in practice and was in pole position. I distinctly remember Raymond Mays talking with Rodney Walkerley about it and saying there was no need to worry – it would never make a racing car and would be lucky to last the race.' Walker said he had the most tremendous faith in the car and was mad about the Mays/Walkerley conversation. 'I thought to myself, I'll bloody well show 'em and I'll see all the BRMs and everything else off.' Poor Rob. Tony Brooks took off, but moved only about ten yards before the gearbox smashed. 'I don't think I've ever been nearer to tears,' admits Walker. He kept faith with the car and within six months had taken the Argentine Grand Prix and then won the second world championship race of 1958, Maurice Trintignant pushing it round fastest in the Monaco Grand Prix.

Rob Walker came near to success at Silverstone on numerous occasions. His Connaught was being driven by Tony Rolt in the early 1950s and Tony managed to completely split the might of Maserati and Ferrari. He was in an incredible fourth place when, with ten laps to go, a key in the half shaft broke and put him out of the race. The same car won the speed trials at Ramsgate the very next day – an oblong screwdriver having been cut in half, made into a key and fitted into the half shaft. It was Tony Rolt again in Walker's Delage in the flooded and abandoned *Daily Express* race. As the 159 Alfas were getting water in their blowers and having terrible trouble keeping going, Tony in the Delage raced past and was lying sixth when it was all called off.

For a long time Rob Walker's number one driver was Stirling Moss, who himself had many experiences at Silverstone. There was the time he was having a glorious dice with Innes Ireland when the rear suspension broke at high speed. The wheels hung out, but Stirling was all right. Then there was the famous occasion when he clouted one of the new Aston Martin Formula 1 cars right in front of the Aston Martin pit. Moss, in the wet, had been pulling out after leaving the paddock and spun in a puddle. The Aston Martin was completely written off, as was Moss's Cooper Climax. Rob Walker said it was one of his most embarrassing moments. 'I remember I apologised profusely to David Brown of Aston Martin and offered to pay for it. I must say I don't think I would have offered to pay if I hadn't been pretty certain that David Brown wouldn't accept the offer. And of course he, fortunately for me, didn't.'

Walker shares the view with many people that Woodcote is probably the greatest corner in the world . . . 'the way they suddenly come shooting round there and you see them burst forth.' One of the never-to-be-forgotten moments was the sight of Mike Hawthorn coming out and practically losing the Ferrari, running almost the full length of the pits on the grass at the far side.

Many memories are of circuit incidents, among them the sight of Jackie Stewart crashing into the bank before the grandstand when he punctured at more than 100 mph. The car was a write off, but Jackie promptly stepped out and got into another car and went on driving just as fast as if nothing at all unusual had happened.

Nor who could forget the time Trintignant's wheel came off his Simca Gordini? It spun high in the air and came crashing down through the roof of a nearby marquee, practically killing a man who was standing there sipping his beer. It was a miracle several people were not killed.

Remember Jo Bonnier's Brabham BRM? Mechanics had been working day and night for a week or more and it still was not ready for the start of practice. Eventually they got it out and off Bonnier went. When he came round and passed the pits for the first time, to the watching team's horror the whole of the rear of the car was on fire. By the time he got down as far as Copse it was blazing madly. Jo pulled off. The fire extinguisher failed to put out the fire and Jo himself dashed for a second.

Silverstone's access and dispersal was no worse than anywhere else. The vast volume of cars and people just made it seem worse. A memory of Rodney Walkerley's is of the stretch of road from Buckingham and a number of enthusiasts rushing ahead of the queue, double banking, waving crash helmets out of car windows and shouting 'Stirling Moss: Make Way!' There must have been at least forty Stirlings that morning.

At one early Silverstone meeting two Russians came to see how motor racing was organised and run at international level, giving rise to the idea that the USSR might enter Grand Prix racing, but nothing more came of it. In the late 1950s a major feature of the pit area was Tony Vandervell's immense Pullman-size caravan with its own detachable tractor to pull it. He used it for entertaining on a lavish scale. The caravan had been built, Walkerley seems to think, for the Gaekwar of Baroda to hunt tigers. Tony was, of course, one of the original consortium to build the BRM but became so impatient with its slow progress that he decided to build the Vanwall on his own.

The memories of people and incidents crowd back. In the pioneering days a great deal of pre-race tomfoolery went on, one of the biggest jokers of them all being that great character, the late Sir Algernon Guinness. He was always incredibly mischievous which at times bordered on the downright risky. On one occasion he arrived during practice and for a joke – and to the consternation of everyone present – drove his old Austin 10 across the track while practice was in progress!

Tall, burly, and ruddy complexioned, Philip Fotheringham-

Parker was one of the early Silverstone drivers whose charming wife Rosemary, known to practically everyone as Georgie, was always in the thick of things. On one occasion she gained the admiration of everyone with a remarkable display of self-control and character. She was on telephone duty in race control when the message came through that her husband had crashed. It would have been so easy to panic and everyone would have understood, but Georgie calmly wrote down the message and fed the instructions through without fuss so that the appropriate emergency action could be taken quickly. Desmond Scannell and others remember being immensely impressed by her action.

Silverstone was gaining in status and it was the habit to try to persuade the big names from abroad to attend – by no means easy. Nuvolari, that great Italian star of motor cycles as well as motor cars, was once persuaded to appear at Silverstone. Food rationing was still in existence and lunch had been arranged for him and his secretary at a hotel in Buckingham. He complained of being unwell at the time and certainly appeared less than fit, but the elaborate meal prepared by an Italian chef proved too tempting and, ill or not, the great man put away an enormous bowl of spaghetti.

Scannell tried hard to persuade Enzo Ferrari to visit Silverstone. He talked to him at Modena, phrasing his request with appropriate humility; 'Would you not honour us by visiting Silverstone for a race?' Ferrari thought for just a moment, then quietly replied: 'You know the Pope? If you want to see him you go to him.' Slight pause. 'If you want to see Ferrari . . .' The rest did not need saying, and Ferrari never did come to Silverstone.

The circuit created its own heroes. Moss in car Number 7 was a popular figure, as were Fangio, Gonzales and Hawthorn, among others, and always closely associated with the circuit. Many of the teams in the early 1950s were run on a shoe-string and the general lack of finance was accepted as an inevitable part of motor racing in those days. Silverstone had not by then had the time to build its reputation for integrity and honesty and one team in particular always insisted on being paid out there and then. Though a little unusual and from an administrative point of view a trifle inconvenient, such were the times that their demands were not considered grossly irregular.

Memories of money brings to mind Graham Hill. It was at Silverstone that John Cooper strode up to Graham in the pits and, talking terms, asked him if £100 would do. Graham said he almost fell backwards. He did not know that much starting money was offered to anyone, let alone himself. Graham has many tales to tell of Silverstone and in his book *Life at the Limit* explains how he would often make it a family occasion at Silverstone, because of the Doghouse Club there: 'The club is properly known as the Women's Motor Racing Associates Club and is for the wives, girl friends and anyone connected with motor racing. They do a lot of charity work and run a splendid hospitality service.'

Hill tells this charming tale: 'On one occasion Bett sent Brigette, then about four, off to the race office to collect some results sheets and lap charts; off she toddled, arrived eventually at the race office and asked for the documents. The officials, of course, wanted to know who they were for and who she might be: "They're for my daddy," she told them and when asked who he was said: "Well, they call him Graham Hill." '

Silverstone set completely new and revolutionary standards for race organisation and such services as first aid, race control, commentators, press facilities and so on. Scannell vividly recalls his visit in the mid-1950s to the Belgian Grand Prix. As an official he enquired about first aid arrangements. He was three quarters of an hour trying to locate the first aid post and, once there, found nobody in attendance and no equipment available.

One memorable occasion at the track was the late Lord Howe's 70th birthday, celebrated in the late 1950s. He had served the BRDC as President for more than 25 years and as a surprise, a tent was transformed into a museum with Howe's old Bugatti and pictures of early races, and everything gaily decorated. His old mechanic came along. The old man was taken in to be greeted by Lady Howe. He was overwhelmed by it all. It was a touching moment.

Silverstone's qualities endure. Among the boy scouts called in to help in the early days was a lad called John Pearson. He was dedicated to motor racing and after going into the army and coming out again, became Silverstone's Driver of the Year. The association continued right into the 1970s with John's name appearing in programmes.

F

Timekeeping was something of a problem in the early days. Des Scannell, then secretary of the BRDC and Clerk of the Course, imported his old friend from Ireland, Pop Wright and his own team, to do the job. Pop used to leave his watch running and read off the times aloud, somewhat to the vexation of the RAC timekeepers. It was not all that accurate, but very quick and perhaps near enough. He did however seem to record a surprisingly large number of drivers with the same times – Ascari and Bira in 1949; Farina and Fangio in 1950; Whitehead and Hawthorn (1952); Hawthorn and Graffenried (1953); and, most unlikely of all, Gonzalez, Moss, Marimon, Fangio, Hawthorn, Ascari and Behra, all equal with 1 min 50 sec in the epic 1954 RAC Grand Prix – not a decimal point between them!

Off track entertainment was almost as riotous as the scenes at the circuit. After their first Silverstone meeting the BRDC gave a dinner for the foreign drivers at an address in Piccadilly. It went with such a swing that when the entertainer made his entry, a new chap who was appearing at the Windmill, no one took any notice. After three exits and re-entrances, he shouted into the rowdy audience: 'Well if you don't want to hear me I might as well pack up and go home.' It was Jimmy Edwards, who ended the evening a great favourite. He eventually had his audience in fits of laughter and, it is alleged by members present at the time, capped his act by playing a euphonium with his nose!

The late Billy Cotton, famous bandleader for many years, was a staunch friend of Silverstone and as a racing driver and BRDC member himself used to organise entertainment for the club. That other celebrated bandleader, Johnny Claes from Belgium, was also very popular at Silverstone and was known to chase observers across a ploughed field on the inside of the track in his bright yellow Talbot.

Strangely, a variety of memories concern the nature of the early lavatories. Rodney Walkerley remembers the girl at an early meeting who endured the agonies of nature because, having visited the 'ladies' she came out in horror and made do between two parked cars. The toilets were then simply canvas screens around a trench with a pole.

Rodney also tells of the time (and maintains it is true) when Robin Richards was broadcasting for the BBC. As he was isolated, he had a small stock of beer in his commentary box on top of the tottering and lofty scaffold-tower. The nearby observers post knew this. Because of his isolated position, he also used an empty beer bottle for obvious reasons. Just as he came on the air he heard someone climbing up his ladder. A hand came into view at floor level, clawed round the door and reached out for his special bottle, apparently half full of 'beer'. Robin, in full song at the microphone, could do nothing. At the last moment, as the bottle was about to be steathily withdrawn, he managed to kick it out of that hand. There was the sound of an oath from outside, vividly expressed, which Robin thinks must have been heard, together with the crash of the bottle, by millions of listeners.

14

Silverstone Today . . .
and Tomorrow

Since the RAC first contemplated Silverstone's desolate wartime airfield as a place to race motor cars, the circuit has gone through many changes. The track has been completely resurfaced; bends are wider now and have been eased to give drivers more control. Facilities for spectators, drivers, mechanics and journalists, primitive in the extreme to begin with, have been much improved.

Even so, at the turn of the decade the most exciting and dramatic changes still lay ahead for in 1972 the BRDC, through its subsidiaries Silverstone Circuits Ltd and Silverstone Leisure Ltd., announced major development plans for transforming the 700 acres of the Silverstone estate into a vast leisure and recreational centre with a still further improved race circuit central to the whole scheme.

But more of that later. With the coming of the 1970s Silverstone prepared for the celebration of its Silver Jubilee in 1973 and, even more immediately, to make improvements at the circuit. As Silverstone Circuits Ltd Chairman Peter Clark put it: 'We continue almost constantly to move vast volumes of earth in order that an ever increasing number of people can have the best possible view of the largest possible amount of circuit. We are constantly improving the entrances and internal roadways. At any given moment there are likely to be literally dozens of improvement projects of one kind or another on hand.'

An ambitious three-year safety improvement programme was begun in 1971 and included steel mesh netting in front of the grandstands to protect spectators from flying debris in the event of a crash, a protective wall of sleepers erected vertically in front of the earth banks and faced with Armco steel barrier (this was extended month by month until the entire circuit on the outside had been equipped) and the filling in of all ditches.

By 1970 speeds continued to reach upwards, aided by remarkable improvement in tyres, and big-time motor racing had become even more spectacular with the infusion of sponsorship of the major events and racing teams. Sponsorship itself was not new. Petrol firms and tyre makers had been doing it for years and Shell, it will be remembered by keen motor racing historians, provided fuel and service centres for the remarkable Peking-Paris race way back in 1907. During the '60s some of the traditional sponsors withdrew, while others continued and in the early 1970s were joined by new big-time spenders, among whom were Players, Rothmans, Yardley and Marlboro.

Silverstone's big International Trophy Race was already sponsored – in 1971, as the year before, by the GKN Group, and, not without justification, the RAC were concerned about the future of the illustrious British Grand Prix. Thus, in 1971 they allowed Silverstone to register yet another 'first' in motor racing with the hosting of the first-ever sponsored British Grand Prix.

The International Wool Secretariat, who had already given support to Sir Francis Chichester's lone voyage round the world, Sheila Scott's international aviation exploits, Prince Michael of Kent in the London-Mexico World Cup rally and Roger Clark in the London-Sydney marathon, now linked their Woolmark symbol to the British Grand Prix in what one journalist described as the biggest soft sell operation in the country's motor racing history. 'It is the fact that the glamour, romance and thrills of our modern equivalent to Roman chariot racing can sell anything from tea to perfumery that brought the International Wool Secretariat on the scene to sponsor the race and call it the Woolmark British Grand Prix.'

As the purists and traditionalist shielded themselves from the inevitable, the IWS prepared to use the privileges their money had given them: mobile billboards by the starting grid; the pure new wool symbol on posters, programmes and much other printed and publicity material; a special Woolmark trophy for the winner.

In a way the sponsors became the new stars of the motor racing world. The public responded to their gay trackside advertising, hospitality caravans, advertisement emblazoned racing cars, long-legged dolly girls, and handout windscreen stickers and giveaways. The sense of excitement and occasion was greater, even if glossier and more superficial.

By 1972 an estimated £7 million was being spent on sport sponsorship, £3 million going on motor racing. Players were said to head the list, spending the bulk of a massive appropriation (though involved in more than twenty other sponsorship ventures) on motor racing.

Early in the year Players announced that Gold Leaf Team Lotus, which they had sponsored for the past three years, would be painted in new colours of black and gold and named after a new cigarette – the John Player Special. In addition they would sponsor what would become known as the John Player Grand Prix, an event which came to Silverstone for the first time in 1973.

Motor racing, like everything else, was caught up in changing times. The character of the sport was on the move. Famous racing drivers were appearing less frequently; some had disappeared altogether to make way for new and younger stars. No longer was a Briton in the driving seat automatically supreme. Chris Amon in his F1 March 701 was the overall winner in the 22nd International Trophy Meeting of 1970 with Mike Hailwood receiving trophies as the winning Formula 5000 driver. The 'Fastest Lap in Practice' winners were old stager Jack Brabham and the sensational Jochen Rindt. It was Jack's last season as a racing driver. He had won the International Trophy race four times, in 1959, '64, '66 and '69.

In 1969 Graham Hill had been flung out of his Lotus at 150 mph while driving in the United States Grand Prix and for some time his career as a racing driver hung in the balance. But Graham in 1971, now nudging the veteran stakes, was back at Silverstone to win the International Trophy.

In 1971 RAC chairman Wilfrid Andrews suggested that motor racing may well be on the threshold of a new era, symbolised perhaps by the retirement the year before of Silverstone favourite Jack Brabham. 'It seems that with him went the domination which British cars and drivers have enjoyed in the World Championship during the past decade or so,' he said. Certainly, the entry lists for that '71 Grand Prix suggested a changing pattern.

The British Team Lotus had a Swede and a Brazilian as works

drivers. Established favourites and former World Champions Graham Hill, John Surtees, Jackie Stewart and Denny Hulme were present, but alongside were exciting newcomers like the Belgian Jacky Ickx, Switzerland's Clay Regazzoni and the Italian-American Mario Andretti who, along with drivers like Fittipaldi, Reine Wisell, Tim Schenken, Francois Cevert, Jo Siffert, Ronnie Peterson, Jean-Pierre Beltoise, Henri Pescarolo and others, made the Woolmark Grand Prix more open and more cosmopolitan than for years. Though not present at the International Trophy, the familiar blood-red Ferraris had returned to racing during the latter half of the previous season to give an exciting account of themselves and provide old motor racing enthusiasts with an opportunity to dig up the old days.

Despite the financial wranglings which at times threatened the World Championship scene, Silverstone came roaring confidently into 1973 with a spectacular programme of events to celebrate its Silver Jubilee. Most important would be the John Player Grand Prix on July 14. Other major occasions included the now-traditional GKN-*Daily Express* Trophy meeting on April 7 and 8, the Martini International 'Interserie' Meeting on May 19–20; a Formula 5000 International on August 5 over the short club circuit; the John Player International motor cycle meeting on August 11–12; the RAC's Tourist Trophy as the British round in the European Touring Challenge on September 23, and a dozen rounds of various National Championships throughout the year.

Curtain raiser to this special year in Silverstone's history was the Silver Jubilee International Trophy Meeting. It captured all the flavour of really big-time motor racing in the 1970s with a programme of events extending over two days.

Support races were a Formula 3 Championship event, attracting drivers from all over Europe together with the best from Britain; a round in the RAC British Touring Car Championship with Frank Gardner's fabulous 7 litre Chevrolet Camaro on show with his sights set to shatter the existing 111 mph saloon car record; Formula Ford – an event counting in the STP Formula Ford Championship; and the fascinating JCB Historic Car Championship with historic sports cars and racing cars speeding round the Silverstone circuit.

Early arrivals could buy hot breakfasts at four points round the circuit from 7 am onwards, and during the day extensive trade areas gave visitors the opportunity to browse around many displays of interest to the motorist and race-goer. A limited number of souvenir post covers had been specially prepared to commemorate the Silver Jubilee Year, and other off-track features included plans for the launching of the Budget Rent-a-Car hot air balloon 'Lady Budget'.

Behind this ambitious programme was the special atmosphere of Silver Jubilee year with streamers and flags and all the other gay paraphenalia to keep the occasion very much in everyone's mind.

Silver Jubilee year was one of the busiest and most exciting twelve months ever experienced by Silverstone. The peak was reached in July with the John Player Grand Prix, the best-promoted race ever to take place in Britain. For months before the public was left in no doubt that if they were not at Silverstone on July 14 they would be missing something very special indeed. John Player's promotional machine billed it as the biggest Grand Prix programme ever seen in Europe. 'There'll be over seven hours of racing, highlight of the day will be the John Player Grand Prix, the only British event to contribute points towards the World Championship. The full-day's programme will include events for Formula 3, Formula Atlantic, Group 2 saloons and Historic cars, with the first race starting at around 11 am.'

No comparable effort had ever before been made to make a day at Silverstone a day out for the whole family. Said one report. 'While dad is enjoying the high-speed thrills of Saturday's John Player Grand Prix at Silverstone motor racing track, mum and the kids can be having a good time too. For a number of off-track activities have been arranged at the race for all the family.'

For those more interested in the racing the event came at an exciting and crucial stage in the World Championship year – just over half way through with Jackie Stewart and Emerson Fittipaldi engaged in a neck-and-neck struggle. At the beginning of the season, Fittipaldi had raced ahead to give the feeling that 1973 could well be his second consecutive World Championship year. He roared to victory in the Argentine and Spain, but Jackie Stewart responded with spectacular wins in South Africa, Belgium and Monaco to put him in the lead by a single point on the eve of Silverstone.

Moreover, the same margin separated the John Player Lotus

Team of Fittipaldi from Stewart's Tyrrell team, the latter trailing in this particular chase.

Jackie also came to Silverstone's John Player Grand Prix poised on the verge of another landmark. It could give him his 26th Grand Prix victory to beat the record of 25 held by the late Jim Clark.

If this was not enough, the year itself had been one of the most volatile in the entire recent history of Grand Prix racing. Early in the year entrants and organisers had been locked in combat over prize money and each Grand Prix in turn had at one time or another appeared to be threatened with cancellation. The John Player Grand Prix was no exception.

But the speculation, fireworks and 'key issues' which had heralded the race were quickly forgotten in the face of the drama and spectacle of the Grand Prix itself. After one lap Jody Scheckter's Yardley McLaren went out of control on the exit from Woodcote, slewed across the track and thundered into the pit wall. A multi-car pile-up followed and forced the authorities to stop the race. It was a move unprecedented in Grand Prix racing in this country. Andrea de Adamich was trapped in his Brabham Ford for some forty minutes but was pulled out somewhat shaken but suffering from nothing more serious than a broken ankle.

Saturday's practice had invested the race with great promise. Former World Champion Denny Hulme set a scorching pace, roaring round the famous circuit at a shattering 137.74 mph, a full second faster than the official lap record. John Player Special Lotus driver Ronnie Peterson was next fastest, ahead of the reigning World Champion Fittipaldi, who shared identical time with Stewart at 1 min 16.9 secs. Roger Williamson, rising young star with plenty of Formula 3 successes to his credit, was set to make his Formula 1 debut in a works March. He spun in practice at well over 100 mph, was innocently involved in the monumental shunt at the beginning of the race, and having survived both hazards, died tragically the very next weekend when he hit a guard rail in the Dutch Grand Prix at Zandvoort and was trapped in the blazing wreckage of his car.

As they came to the grid at Silverstone it was Peter Revson, Denny Hulme and Ronnie Peterson occupying the front positions, with leading World Championship contenders Jackie Stewart and

Emerson Fittipaldi behind. There was a huge crowd, the particular importance and stature of the Grand Prix well evident and Silverstone at its most festive. The carnival atmosphere was accentuated by private aeroplanes, film crew helicopters and the Goodyear blimp, from which the BBC shot some remarkable television film, bringing high altitude views of the famous track never before seen by the viewer.

As the flag dropped Stewart was away like a rocket, moving in close behind leader Ronnie Peterson. As Ronnie drifted a little wide at Maggotts Jackie shot through on the inside and, driving brilliantly, pulled into a distinct lead. At Woodcote he was as much as 100 yards ahead and in the championship battle Jackie had drawn first blood, for Emerson Fittipaldi was well down the field and tending to lose ground rather than gain it.

Through Woodcote and on, roared Stewart, Peterson and the other front runners, but before the race had time to settle it ran headlong into appalling chaos and confusion.

It started as Jody Scheckter challenged Denny Hulme at Woodcote. The former's Yardley McLaren ran out of road, spun on the grass, veered across the track and struck the pit wall. Following cars, travelling at 150 mph, were promptly yanked out of line to avoid Scheckter's stricken car, but the speed was too great and time insufficient. Many simply rammed each other. Crowds at the track and on television watched in horror as one accident followed another, building up within seconds into a scene of devastation never before witnessed at Silverstone. Drivers leaped clear. Prompt and commendable action by marshals prevented any further deterioration of the scene as drivers approaching Woodcote received appropriate signals.

Six of the eight extensively damaged cars had to be written off. The great crowd was stunned. Cars, twisted and torn, littered the track. Miraculously, no one was seriously hurt, but the race was not resumed for 1½ hours because of the need to free Andrea de Adamich, trapped for some forty minutes in his Brabham, and to clear up the mess. Silverstone's well-trained fire and rescue teams were quickly in action and worked well, while the prompt decision of the RAC's Director of Motor Sport, Dean Delamont, in stopping the race was fully justified. The accident vindicated the latest safety regulations, the new 'deformable' cars withstanding the impact of collision incredibly well and although all cars were carrying almost a full load of fuel, there was no fire and hardly any leakage onto the track. Not long before, television viewers had seen the construction of these 'deformable structures' in a fascinating behind-the-scenes BBC documentary about Graham Hill's Shadow. It showed how liquid plastic foam is poured in the monocoque structure, where it expands to occupy every space within the fuel tank compartment. It then becomes solid to form an extremely light yet effective protection against fuel tank rupture in an accident and thereby reducing the chance of fire from escaping fuel.

The race was re-started ninety minutes later with a somewhat depleted field. It says much for the racing that, in spite of the drama of a couple of hours before, the Grand Prix was by no means an anti-climax. Drivers displayed great courage as they handled their cars without inhibition in a sparkling race full of interest. Stewart again tried to lead from the start, but this time was unsuccessful. Meantime, Ronnie Peterson had rushed to the front and was intent on holding station. Jackie was in third position, with Fittipaldi roaring up in fourth. Thoughts turned again to the championship battle and how vital the race was to these two drivers. As it happened the championship battle was hardly ever an issue. Stewart was in second position by lap 2 and was challenging Peterson strongly on lap 5 when he lost control at Stowe, spinning into the infield. He re-started well down the field and never fully recovered, being forced into the pits on lap 10 and finishing the race in tenth position.

As he pulled out of the race Stewart must have glanced in desperation at Fittipaldi's position, for at this stage the latter was handily placed, some 5 seconds behind leader Peterson. Stewart's cause slumped further as Emerson reduced the lead to fractionally over 3 seconds by lap 20. At half distance, Peter Revson closed behind Fittipaldi, who was followed by Denny Hulme and then new boy James Hunt in a March 731.

Two more laps and Jackie could count his blessings as Fittipaldi went out of the race at Abbey Curve with a broken drive-shaft. No points therefore for either driver, as the World Championship top positions remained unchanged.

The battle was now between Revson, challenging strongly, and Peterson for lead position, but Hunt drove a great race and on lap 38 took Hulme to move into third position. Lap 39 and

Revson moved into the lead. Hotly pursued later by Peterson, he held on to cross the line first. Meantime, old stager Hulme was not prepared to let upstart Hunt have the race all his own way and on lap 56 re-took third position, struggled to hold it, and did so.

In an exciting, sliding finish, American Peter Revson in his Yardley McLaren with the four year-old V8 Ford Cosworth engine, recorded his first Formula 1 victory, with Sweden's Ronnie Peterson in the John Player Lotus only fractionally slower. Denny Hulme in another Yardley McLaren held grimly to third position with James Hunt racing into a dramatic fourth place in his first Grand Prix season. Revson's overall average was 131.75 mph and four cars lapped at an average of more than 130 mph.

The 160 mph pile-up filled the papers for days, but when the dust had settled and breathing returned to normal, perhaps the most significant drive of all was seen to have been registered by James Hunt, the 25 year-old Londoner in Lord Hesketh's privately-entered March-Ford.

The John Player Grand Prix gave the Silverstone crowd their full taste of this latest Formula 1 young-man-in-a-hurry. Placed around ninth at the start, he worked through the field to fifth by lap 11 and produced a remarkable performance, in spite of a large piece of rubber missing from a front tyre, to finish in fourth place. The tall, dashing fair-haired stylist, backed by the flamboyant Lord Hesketh, moreover turned in the fastest lap of the race at 134.06 mph.

Though considered as something of an overnight success by the general public, Hunt had laboured longer and harder than many realised. Like so many, his inspiration came from visiting Silverstone on a day which changed the path of his life from medicine to motors. Three years later he bought a Formula Ford on hire purchase and at the end of 1969 was well entrenched in Formula 3 racing with a Brabham BT21. Then came a Lotus 59 and outstanding success.

His fortunes slumped in 1971 while driving a works Formula 3 March and the season is remembered for his retirements and crashes. In 1972 he met Lord Hesketh, scored successes for him in Formula 2 and then moved into Formula 1. Though still to win a Grand Prix, at the time of Silverstone's 1973 Grand

Prix, he was already considered by many as Britain's brightest hope for the future.

While memories were still vivid of this spectacular Silverstone event, motor cycle race fans were keyed up for the major John Player International to take place at the circuit on August 11 and 12. Speed again was the compelling feature and the occasion was advertised by John Player like this: 'You'll see the world's biggest stars from 12 different countries. And some of the fastest motorcycles, like the John Player Nortons, in the fastest race, Formula 750, at Britain's fastest circuit, Silverstone.'

A star entry was headed by Phil Read and Giacomo Agostini and included Barry Sheene and Stan Woods on GB Suzukis, Paul Smart, Jack Findlay, Peter Williams, Dave Croxford and Teuvo Lansivuovi, the flying Finn. And the racing, as recalled in Chapter 8, fully lived up to its promise.

Silverstone had celebrated its Silver Jubilee in sensational style and as the season ran out there were pangs of regret that it was all over.

But the famous circuit and its staunch followers had much still to be excited about, for the track had already announced details of a massive face-lift in which the pits, paddock and grandstands were to be re-styled and the whole area developed as part of a long-term scheme into an ambitious leisure centre. There was talk of an artificial ski-slope, a rallycross circuit, show jumping arena and a caravan park. Meanwhile, circuit manager George Smith, commenting on the circuit itself, said: 'We have improved another threequarters of a mile of spectator banking this year (1973) and built new banks which leaves only about a quarter mile of the circuit not banked.'

Peter Clark, Chairman of Silverstone Circuits Ltd said 'I'm not really very much impressed by all the talk of future possiblities. What we need are some Outline Planning approvals, to enable us to act. Our aim is to have a substantial motel, sophisticated camping and caravanning facilities, plus a varied selection of sporting pastimes at the northern end of the estate. In the wooded areas at the southern end, by contrast, the idea is to cater for the quieter and more gentle types of recreation including horse riding and fishing.'

The overall policy, continued Peter, was to make the Silverstone estate more attractive and beautiful than at present (moving still further away from the desolate wartime airfield atmosphere) and to bring its amenities within the scope of a wider cross-section of the public.

For motor racing followers unnerved by talk of horse riding and motels, camping and fishing, Peter Clark had some consoling news: 'On the motoring side we shall relentlessly continue our efforts to make spectatoring at Silverstone more enjoyable. We shall continue our work aimed at reducing delays suffered by the public on arrival at or departure from our major meetings. To this end we are endeavouring to persuade adjacent land owners to grant us a right of way to the A413 Buckingham/Towcester Road. We hope eventually to have permanent grandstand buildings, incorporating fully adequate bars, restaurants and all other desirable facilities. Motor racing will always remain the top priority in our minds, as is inevitable in view of who we are – the British Racing Driver's Club'.

In the meantime, the circuit continued to be plagued by its location and by circumstance, as in the past. Difficulties and delays in having their ambitious plans accepted were perhaps accentuated by the Bucks/Northants County Boundary passing almost exactly through the middle of the estate, and by the whole fabric of Local Government being, at the time, in a state of upheaval with outgoing councils naturally reluctant to take decisions of which they felt their successors may disapprove.

That Silverstone's ambitious scheme will go through eventually is to be expected because this is fully in keeping with Silverstone's remarkable tradition of survival and triumph over adversity during its first twenty-five years.

Conclusion

For many thousands of motor racing enthusiasts there is no place in the world quite like Silverstone. Created out of nothing, it has been fashioned in the face of extreme and continuing difficulties. Today it stands proudly as the country's traditional home of motor racing and is famous far beyond home shores as much for its prestige and status as for the excitement of its racing.

Not that the latter is ever in short measure at Silverstone. The circuit has attracted all the major marques for more than twenty-five years and the prospect of racing there, with perhaps the outside chance of victory, has brought the best drivers from all over the world to Silverstone. Yet never, despite this, has it lost touch with the grass roots of the sport. The dedicated amateur, the young man out to make a name professionally, the motoring clubs who are the backbone of the sport – all find an instinctive home there.

Silverstone brought international motor racing back to Britain after the war when Brooklands and Donington were no more and prospects looked bleak. It was honoured by a Grand Prix d'Europe, the first to be run by that time outside France and Italy, traditionally the major motor racing nations. It staged many innovations and introduced production sports car racing. The quick-fire programme of events as envisaged by Tom Blackburn and inaugurated by the *Daily Express* International Trophy programmes was a completely new concept in motor racing. The original home of the country's major race, the Grand Prix, and of the most important non-championship event, the International Trophy, Silverstone is also Britain's fastest circuit. Nowhere else in Britain can racing cars be seen travelling at speeds of 180 mph and more in a motor race.

Basil Cardew once described it as the Ascot of motor racing.

Piers Courage played truant from Eton to go there. It was there that Denny Hulme drove his first race in England . . . barefoot! Silverstone inspired many world famous drivers to choose racing as a career; others had their debut there. It is the natural choice when a new car or driver has to be tested or a film crew wants authentic background and atmosphere of big-time motor racing.

Motor racing is perhaps the most dynamic of all sports. The racing car has become a sensitive, complicated, precocious, temperamental thoroughbred piloted by globe-trotting, helmeted headliners who wedge themselves deep into monocoque frames and are famous throughout the world. Yet Silverstone somehow manages to suggest that it has not been totally engulfed by commerce. Along with the intense excitement and spectacle of racing at Silverstone, the gaiety and the carnival presentation, one feels still the sense of history and tradition and something of the earthiness of those glorious pioneering days when motorised gladiators in open chargers sped and spun round a bare, windswept airfield.

Silverstone occupies a unique place, not only in motor racing history but in the affections of motor sport enthusiasts. Past, present and future, with its recently announced plans for exciting further development, it stands as fine testimony to those whose vision created it and to all who have had a hand in its progress.

Appendix 1

THE BRITISH RACING DRIVERS' CLUB

Presidents in Chief	H.R.H. Prince George, The Duke of Kent	

		years
Presidents	The Rt Hon The Earl Howe	1928–1964
	The Hon Gerald Lascelles	1965–

Vice Presidents
(as of August
1973)

P. C. T. Clark; H. W. Cook; J. N. Cooper;
W. M. Couper; S. C. H. Davis; K. D.
Evans; Capt E. T. Eyston, OBE, MC; F. R.
Gerard; Major M. H. Morris-Goodall;
S. C. Moss, OBE; D. J. Scannell, OBE;
R. K. Tyrrell; R. R. C. Walker

		years
Secretaries	H. N. Edwards	1928–1936
	D. J. Scannell, OBE	1936–1956
	J. Eason-Gibson	1956–1968
	A. A. Salmon	1968–

Elected Committee
(as of 1974)

R. Attwood
P. Gaydon
A. D. Gill
P. Jopp
C. Lucas
E. Nelson
D. R. Piper
P. Scott Russell
J. G. S. Sears
D. F. Truman
A. G. Whitehead

Appendix 2

Silverstone Circuits Ltd

Directors:

P. C. T. Clark, Chairman

J. W. Brown, Marketing

The Hon G. D. Lascelles

A. A. Salmon

J. G. S. Sears

Circuit Manager:	George Smith
Press Officer:	Pierre Aumonier
In Charge Testing:	S. Herbert
In Charge Administration:	Mrs Ivy Cakebread
In Charge Bookings:	Miss Carole Hinton

1948
SILVERSTONE GRAND PRIX CIRCUIT

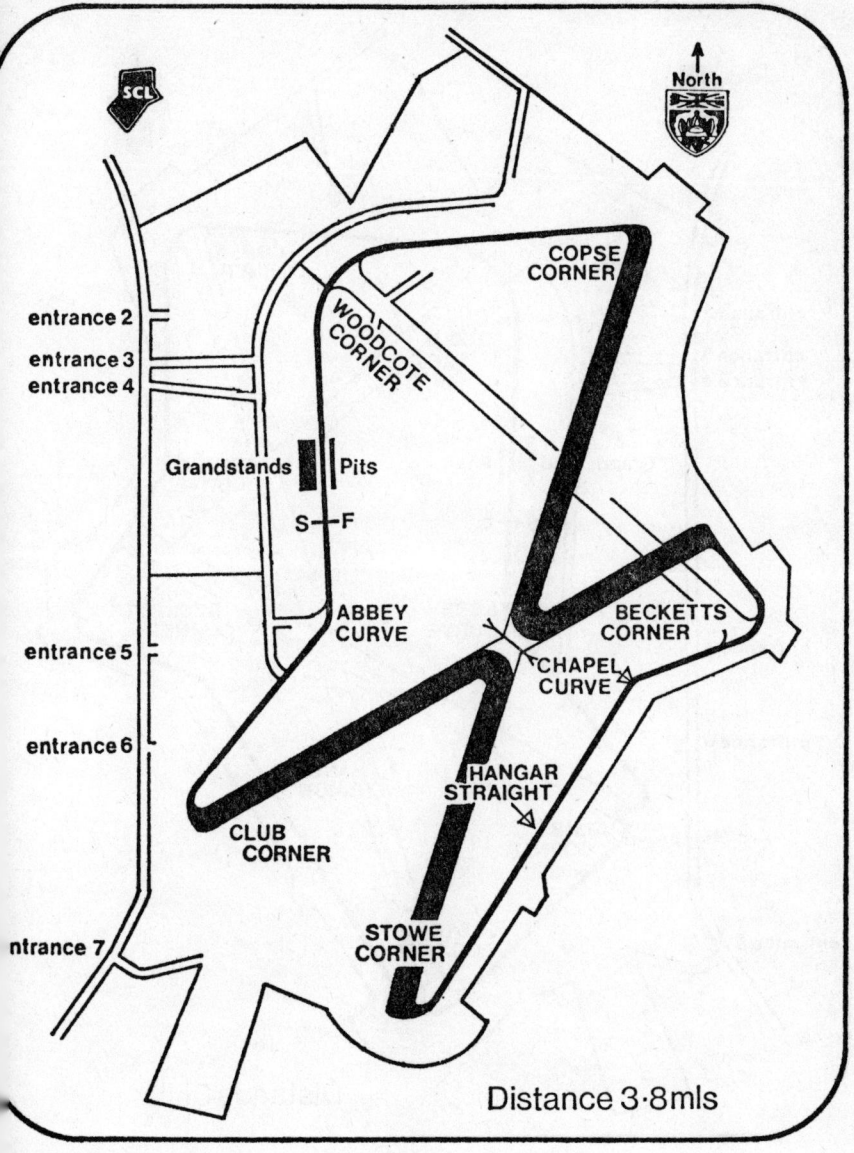

1949
SILVERSTONE GRAND PRIX CIRCUIT

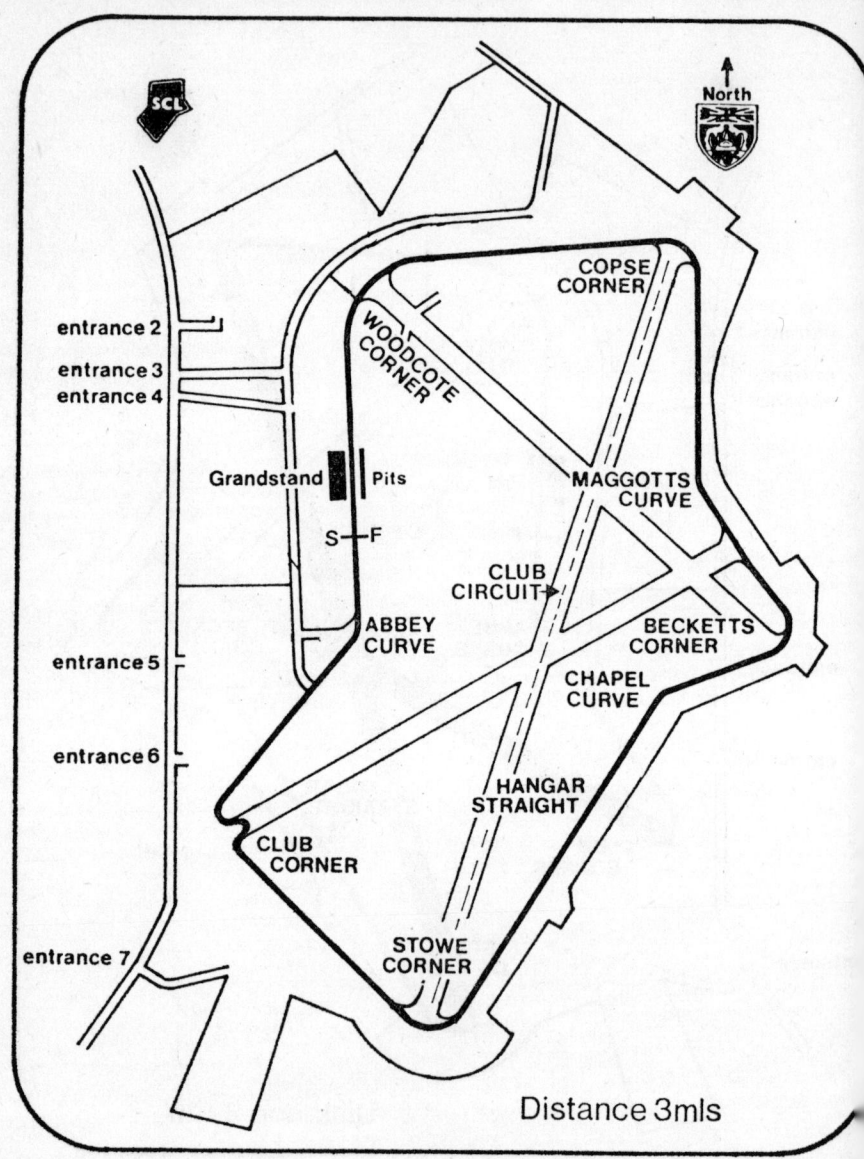

Distance 3mls

1950
SILVERSTONE GRAND PRIX CIRCUIT

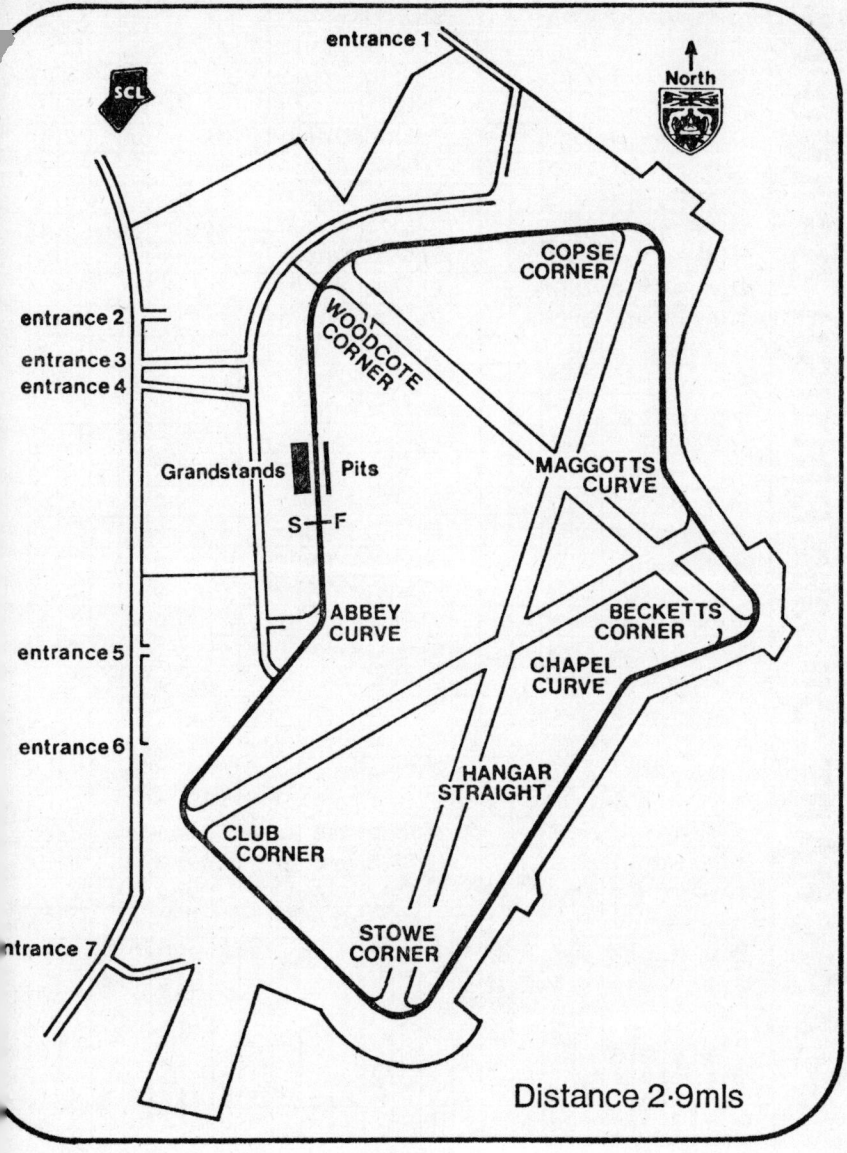

entrance 1

SCL

North

COPSE
CORNER

WOODCOTE
CORNER

entrance 2

entrance 3

entrance 4

Grandstands   Pits

MAGGOTTS
CURVE

S — F

ABBEY
CURVE

BECKETTS
CORNER

entrance 5

CHAPEL
CURVE

entrance 6

HANGAR
STRAIGHT

CLUB
CORNER

entrance 7

STOWE
CORNER

Distance 2·9mls

LAP CHART OF 1950 BRITISH GRAND PRIX

No	CAR	DRIVER	1	2	3	4	5	6	7	8	9	10	11	12	13	14	15	16	17	18	19	20	21	22	23	24	25	26	27	28	29	30	31	32	33	34	35
1	A-R.(B)	Fangio	1	1	2	2	2	2	2	1	1	1	2	2	2	1	1	3	3	3	3	3	3	3	3	3	3	1	1	1	3	3	3	3	2	2	2
2	A-R.(R)	Farina	3	3	1	1	1	1	1	3	3	2	1	1	1	2	2	2	2	2	1	1	1	1	1	2	2	2	2	2	2	2	2	2	1	1	1
3	A-R.(Y)	Fagioli	2	2	3	3	3	3	3	2	2	4	3	3	3	3	3	1	1	1	2	2	2	2	2	1	1	2	2	2	2	2	2	2	3	3	3
4	A-R.(G)	Parnell	4	4	4	4	4	4	4	4	4	13	4	4	4	4	4	4	4	4	4	4	4	4	4	4	4	4	4	4	4	4	4	4	4	4	4
5	M.	Murray	15	15	15	15	14	14	14	14	14	13	4	13	13	13	13	13	13	13	13	13	13	13	13	18	17	13	13	13	13	13	13	13	13	12	12
6	M.	Hampshire	14	14	14	14	13	13	13	13	13	12	13	12	12	12	12	12	12	12	12	12	12	12	12	12	12	12	12	12	12	12	12	12	12	11	11
7	M.	Hamilton																																			
8	E.R.A.	Johnson	R																																		
9	E.R.A.	Walker	13	13	13	13	R																														
10	M.	Fry	20	20	20	20	19	19	19	19	19	18	18	18	18	18	18	18	18	18	18	18	18	18	18	17	17	17	17	17	17	16	16	16	16	15	15
11	E.R.A.	Harrison	12	12	12	12	12	12	12	12	12	11	10	10	10	10	10	10	10	10	10	10	10	10	10	10	10	10	10	10	10	9	9	9	9	8	8
12	E.R.A.	Gerard	11	11	11	11	11	11	11	11	11	10	11	11	11	11	11	11	11	11	11	11	11	11	11	11	11	11	11	11	10	10	10	10	9	9	9
14	T.	Cabantous	8	8	8	8	8	8	8	8	8	7	7	7	7	7	7	6	6	6	6	6	6	6	6	6	6	6	6	6	6	6	6	5	5	5	5
15	T.	Rosier	9	9	9	9	9	9	9	9	9	8	8	8	8	8	8	8	8	8	8	8	8	8	8	8	8	8	8	8	8	8	8	6	6	6	6
16	T.	Etancelin	10	10	10	10	10	10	10	10	10	9	9	9	9	9	9	9	9	9	9	9	9	9	9	9	9	9	9	9	9	11	11	11	11	10	10
17	T.	Martin	7	7	7	6	6	6	6	6	7	R																									
18	T.	Claes	17	17	17	17	16	16	16	16	15	15	15	15	15	15	15	15	15	15	15	15	15	15	14	14	14	14	14	14	14	14	14	14	14	13	13
19	M.	Chiron	16	16	16	16	15	15	15	15	15	14	14	14	14	14	14	14	14	14	14	14	14	14	P	R											
20	M.	De Graffenried	6	6	6	7	7	7	7	7	6	6	6	6	6	6	6	6	7	7	7	7	7	7	7	7	7	7	7	7	7	7	7	7	7	7	7
21	M.	Bira	5	5	5	5	5	5	5	5	5	5	5	5	5	5	5	5	5	5	5	5	5	5	5	5	5	5	5	5	5	5	5	5	5	R	
22	M.	Bonetto																																			
23	A.	Kelly	19	19	19	18	18	18	18	18	17	17	17	17	17	17	17	17	17	17	17	17	16	16	16	16	16	16	16	16	16	17	16	17	17	16	16
24	A.	Crossley	18	18	18	18	17	17	17	17	17	16	16	16	16	16	16	16	16	16	16	16	16	16	16	15	15	15	15	15	15	15	15	15	15	14	14

A-R. Alfa Romeo   M. Maserati   T. Talbot   A. Alta

166

This page contains a race lap chart (1950 British Grand Prix) showing driver positions for laps 36 to 70.

No	DRIVER	CAR	36	37	38	39	40	41	42	43	44	45	46	47	48	49	50	51	52	53	54	55	56	57	58	59	60	61	62	63	64	65	66	67	68	69	70
1	Fangio	A-R.(B)	2	2	2	2	2	2	2	2	2	2	2	2	2	2	2	2	2	2	2	2	2	2	2	2	2	2	R								
2	Farina	A-R.(R)	1	1	1	1	1	1	1	1	1	1	1	1	1	1	1	1	1	1	1	1	1	1	1	1	1	1	1	1	1	1	1	1	1	1	1
3	Fagioli	A-R.(Y)	3	3	3	3	3	3	3	3	3	3	3	3	3	3	3	3	3	3	3	3	3	3	3	3	3	3	2	2	2	2	2	2	2	2	2
4	Parnell	A-R.(G)	4	4	4	4	4	4	4	4	4	4	4	4	4	4	4	4	4	4	4	4	4	4	4	4	4	4	3	3	3	3	3	3	3	3	3
5	Murray	M.	10	10	10	10	10	10	10	10	10	10	10	10	10	10	10	10	10	10	10	10	10	10	10	10	10	10	10	10	10						
6	Hampshire	M.																																			
7	Hamilton	M.																																			
8	Johnson	E.R.A.																																			
9	Walker	E.R.A.																																			
10	Fry	M.	11	11	11	11	11	11	11	11	11	11	11	11	11	13	13	13	13	13	13	13	13	13	13	13	13	13	15	15	15	15	15	15	15	15	15
11	Harrison	E.R.A.	9	9	9	9	9	9	9	9	9	9	9	9	9	8	8	8	8	8	8	8	8	8	8	8	8	8	7	7	7	7	7	7	7	7	7
12	Gerard	E.R.A.	8	8	8	8	8	8	8	8	8	8	8	8	8	7	7	7	7	7	7	7	7	7	7	7	7	7	6	6	6	6	6	6	6	6	6
14	Cabantous	T.	5	5	5	5	5	5	5	5	5	5	5	5	5	5	5	5	5	5	5	5	5	5	5	5	5	5	4	4	4	4	4	4	4	4	4
15	Rosier	T.	6	6	6	6	6	6	6	6	6	6	6	6	6	6	6	6	6	6	6	6	6	6	6	6	6	6	5	5	5	5	5	5	5	5	5
16	Etancelin	T.	10	10	10	10	10	10	10	10	10	10	10	10	10	10	10	10	10	10	10	10	10	10	10	10	10	10	9	9	9						
17	Martin	T.	12	12	12	12	12	12	12	12	12	12	12	12	12	12	12	12	12	12	12	12	12	12	12	12	12	12	12								
18	Claes	T.																																			
19	Chiron	M.																																			
20	M.De Graffenried	M.	7	7	7	7	7	7	7	7	7	7	7	7	7	R																					
21	Bira	M.	16	16	16	16	16	16	16	16	16	16																									
22	Bonetto	M.																																			
23	Kelly	A.	13	13	13	13	13	13	13	13	13	13	14	14	14	14	14	14	14	14	14	14	14	14	14	14	14	14	15	15	15	15	15	15	15	15	15
24	Crossley	A.	14	14	14	14	14	14	14	R																											

167

1952 onwards

SILVERSTONE GRAND PRIX CIRCUIT

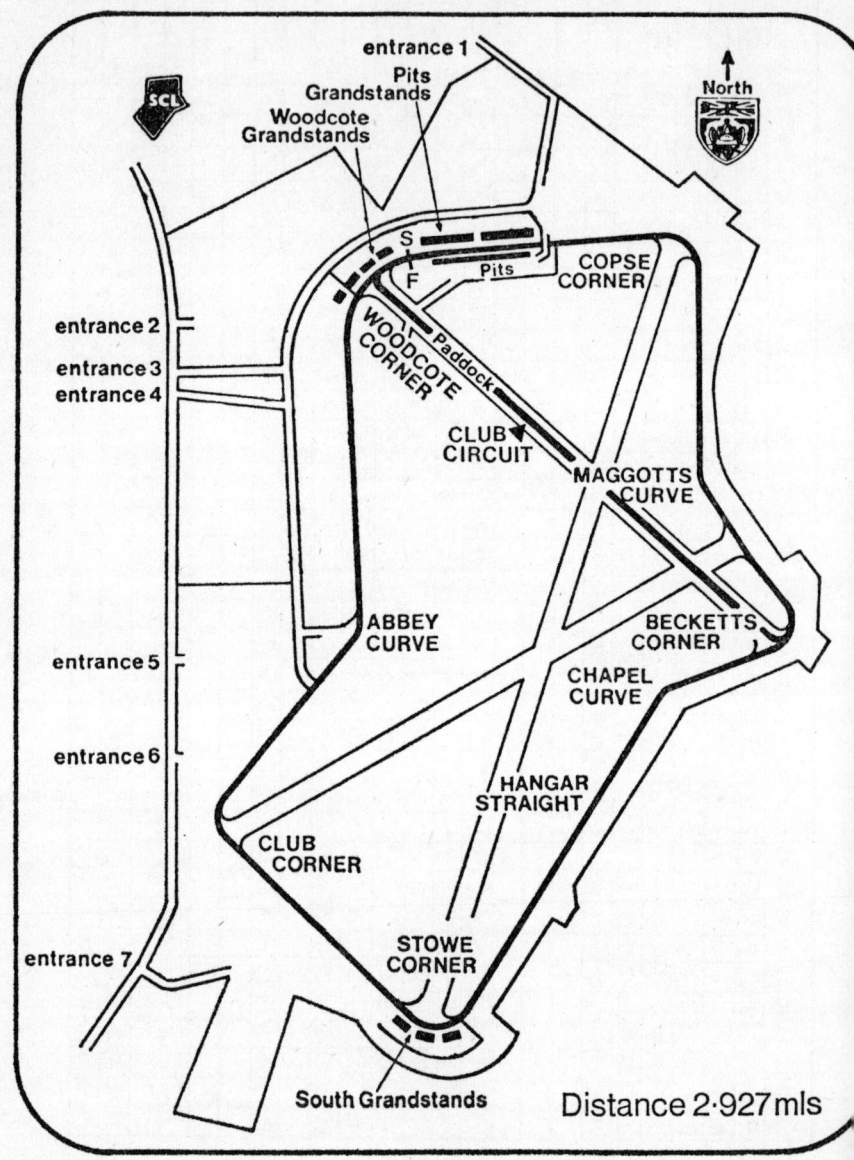

Index